Capturing the Moment
The Art & Science of Photographing Wild Animals

by

Award-Winning Photographer
Kathleen Reeder

Layout and design by urbanartdesign.com

Printed in the United States of America
US Paperback Release: December 2013

This book is dedicated
with boundless gratitude to all wildlife
and to the special people who cherish them as I do.
Both have taught me much about myself,
relationships, beauty and love.

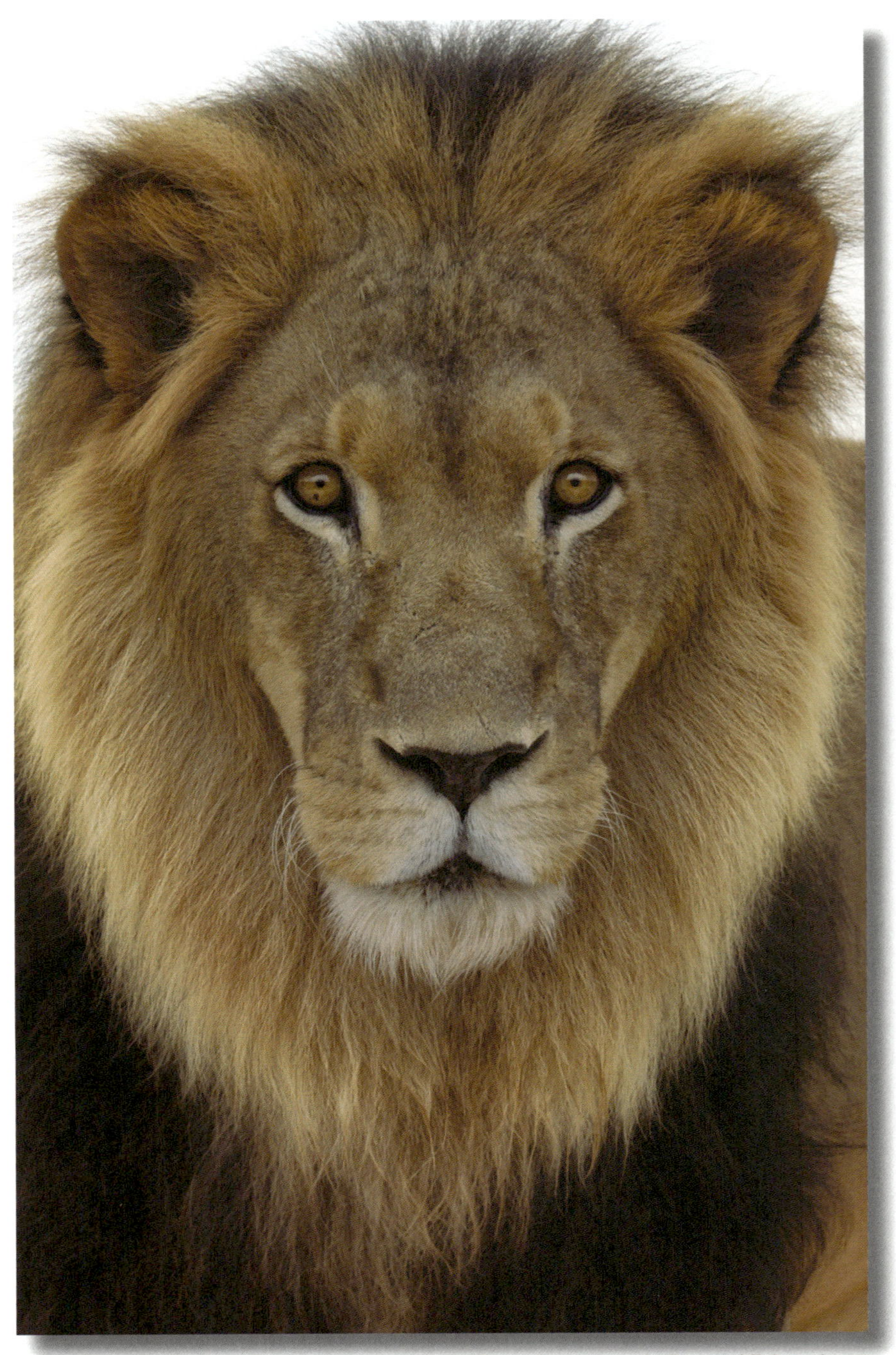

African Lion: Out of Africa Wildlife Park, AZ

TABLE OF CONTENTS

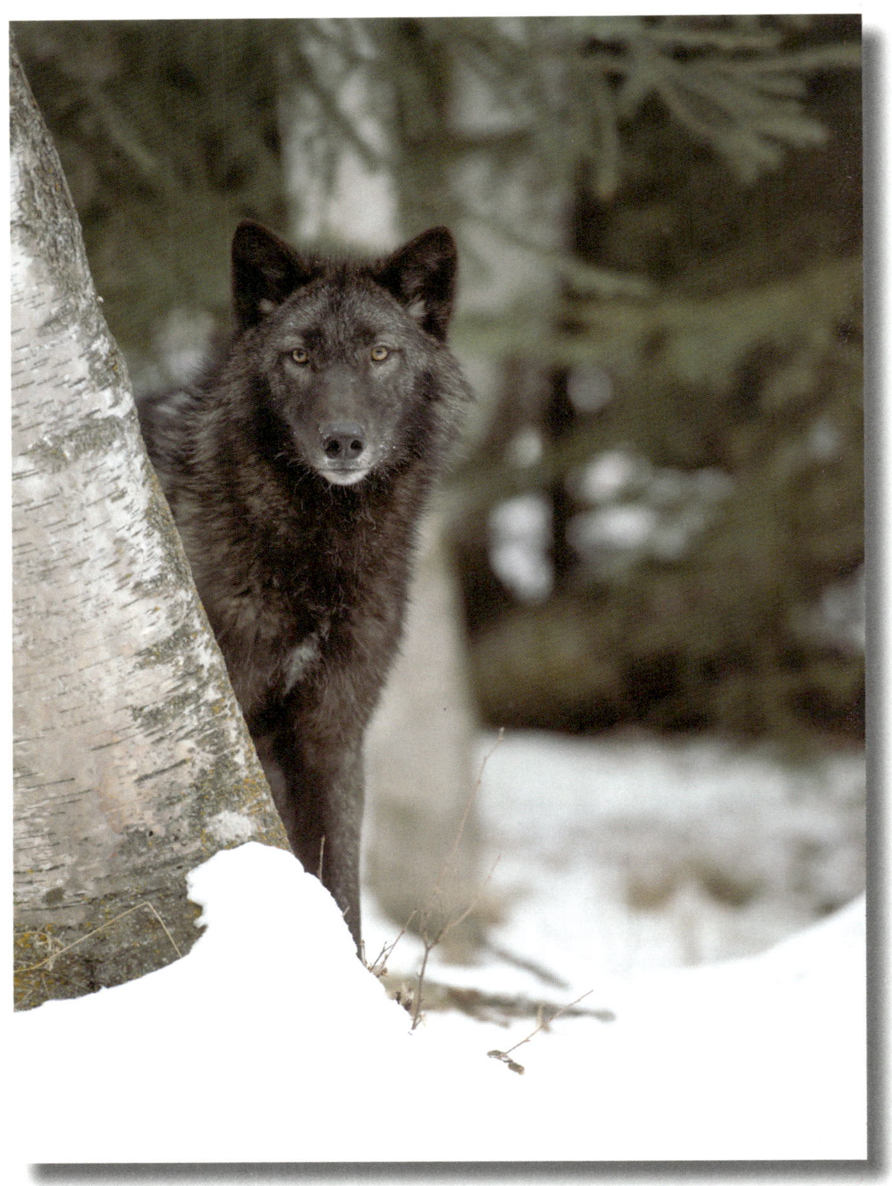

Gray Wolf: Triple D Game Ranch, MT

Introduction

Imagine savoring the experience of an intimate connection between you and a wild animal... and at the same time, capturing that moment in a photograph. Photographing wild animals is one of the most rewarding areas of photography. It touches our emotions, is dynamic and fast moving, and when we allow ourselves to enter an animal's world, the experience changes our lives.

This book will prepare you to take wild animal photos that capture the emotion, the beauty and the thrill. It will benefit photographers of all skill levels, but is geared towards the photographer with a digital SLR camera and basic knowledge of its operation. The book outlines the essential compositional elements for wildlife photography, simplifies the technical knowledge needed to effectively operate your equipment, prepares you for spending a day with wildlife and is compact enough to keep in your camera bag.

Consider the information presented in this book and you will be rewarded with incredible wildlife photographs that people will love. Most of all, the information will enhance your life by documenting your experiences and enable you to relive those special moments when you connect with wildlife.

I organized the content into four sections:

Section 1: Capturing an Intriguing Composition
Section 2: Preparing to Photograph Wildlife
Section 3: Picking the Optimal Camera Settings
Section 4: Setting Up On Location

The sections are presented in the order of their importance. I feel that *Capturing an Intriguing Composition* is the most important; therefore, it is outlined first. This first section is the "Art" of capturing an excellent photograph. The remaining sections in the book are the "Science."

Some of you may ask why I feel that the "Art" is more important than the "Science." It is more important to me for I believe it is through the composition that you share the heart and soul of a wild animal. The composition is how you show your appreciation and love for that animal. An excellent composition will reveal what was experienced up close, in that one moment--feeling the exhilaration and connection to a live animal. The "Science" is the nuts and bolts information, which of course one must master; but it is the compositional techniques that enable you to communicate the essence and spirit of an animal.

** Some of the photos in this book were taken at wildlife sanctuaries, rescues, national parks, preserves, and zoos where our precious wildlife have loving, safe and protected environments. Please remember to donate to these organizations in order to support the on-going care of the animals, some which are facing extinction. Thank you.*

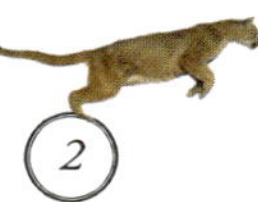

Capturing an Intriguing Composition

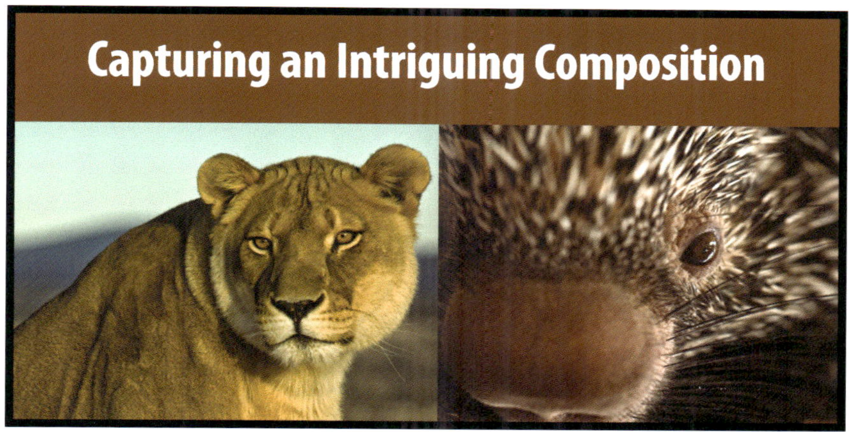

This section includes 9 guidelines:

1) Aim for Eye Level Perspective
2) Catch the Animal's Behavior
3) Wait for a Pose
4) Provide Room for the Subject to Move in the Frame
5) Keep Backgrounds Simple
6) Apply the Rule of Thirds
7) Photograph Wildlife in the Best Light
8) Use Color for Impact
9) Respect Their World

1) Aim for Eye Level Perspective: With wildlife photography, the most effective perspective is obtained at the subject's eye level. You have probably heard the saying, "The eyes are the window to the soul." By photographing at eye level, you are sharing a moment inside the animal's world. To create an engaging photo, make sure the eyes are open and in sharp focus.

Portraits look even better if you are able to get the glint of light reflecting off of the eyes. (See lioness and porcupine above.)

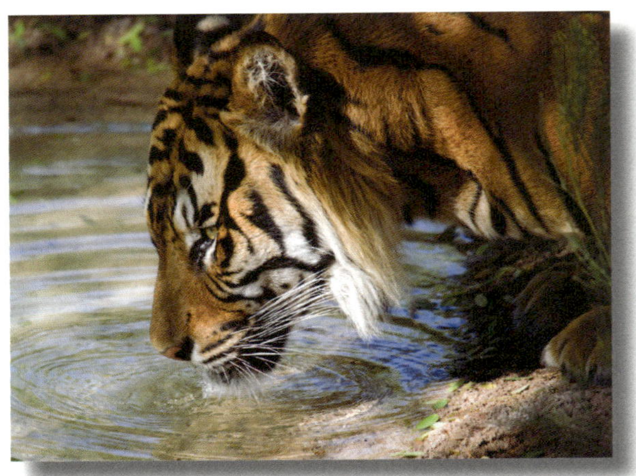

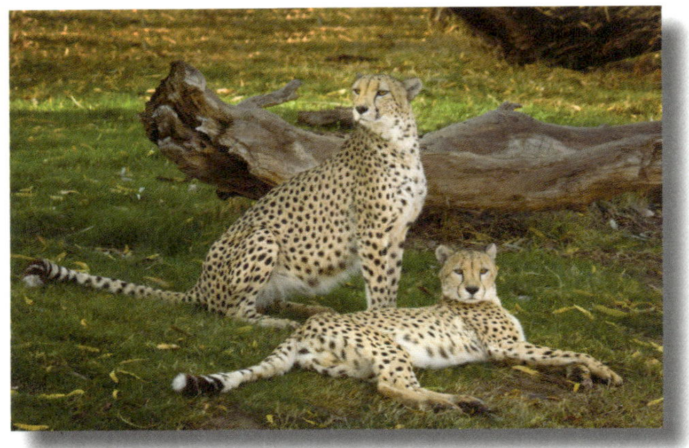

Sumatran Tiger:
Phoenix Zoo, AZ

Cheetahs:
Phoenix Zoo, AZ

Snow Leopard:
Triple D Game Ranch, MT

(Opposite Page) Eurasian Eagle Owl:
AZ-Sonora Desert Museum

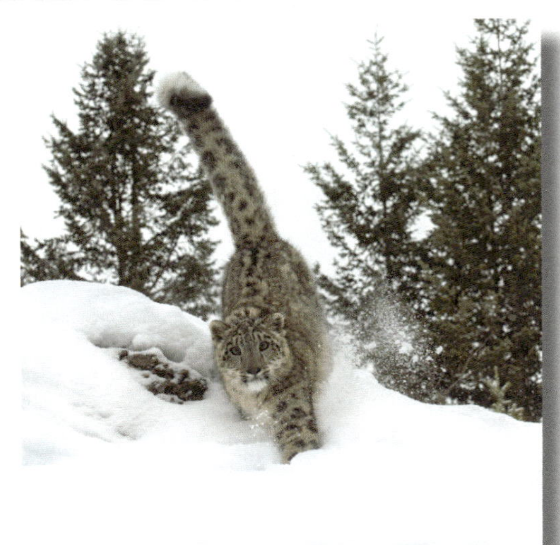

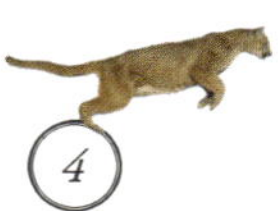

In addition to sharpness, capturing the whites of an animal's eyes adds adorableness and vulnerability to an animal.

When the eyes are out of focus or shadowed, the photo does not convey a connection to the animal and has less impact.

2) Catch the Animal's Behavior: The best photographs are those that exhibit behavior. Look for moments that tell a story and your wildlife photos will have more impact.
Examples are:

* *Action (running, hunting, fishing, fighting, flying, climbing, singing, stretching, yawning, preening)*

* *Interaction (grooming each other, infants at play, squabbling, mating)*

* *Family portraits*

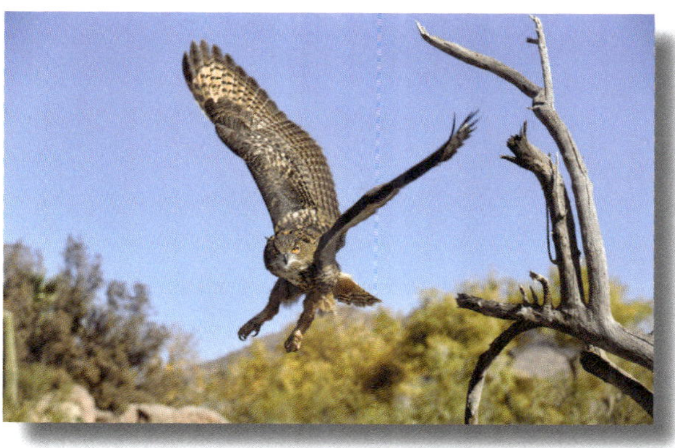

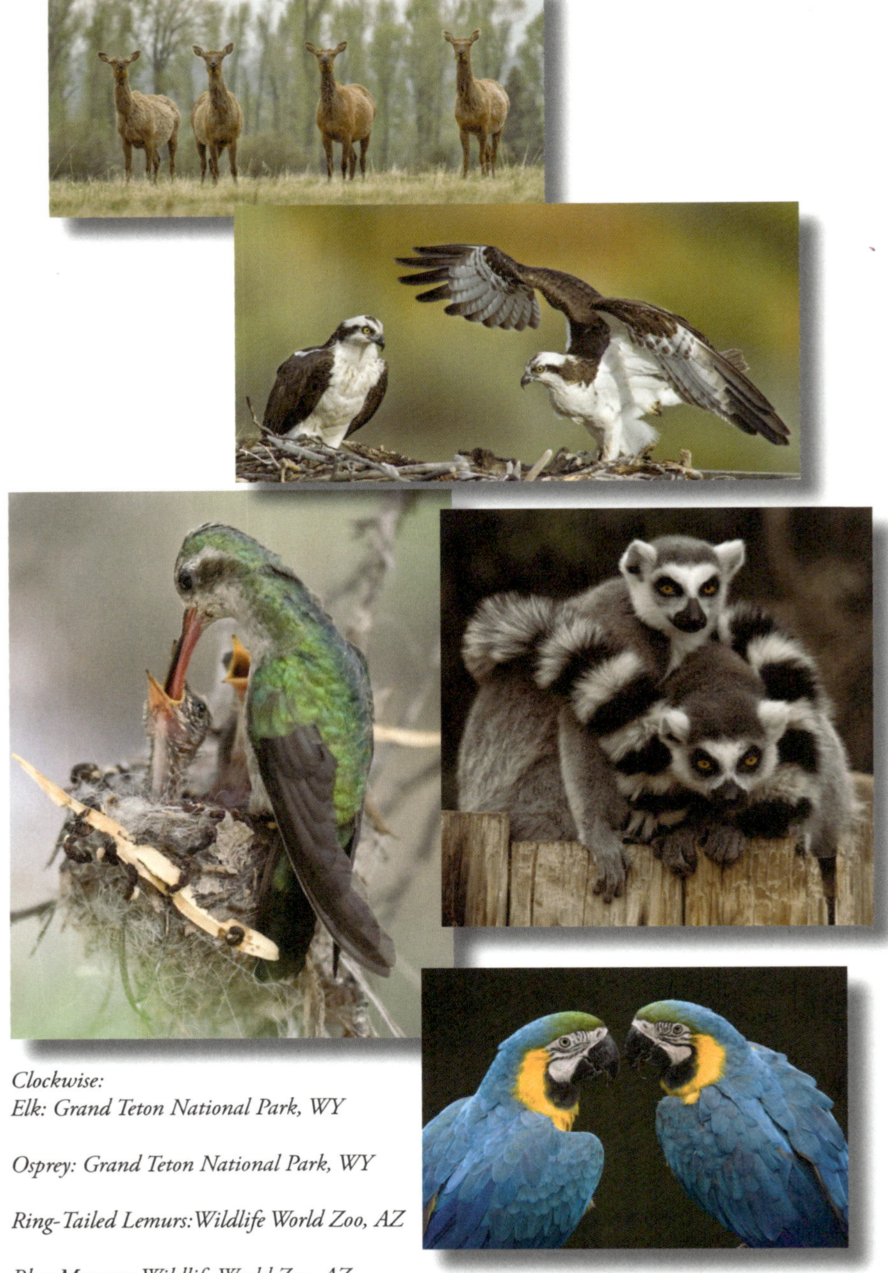

Clockwise:
Elk: Grand Teton National Park, WY

Osprey: Grand Teton National Park, WY

Ring-Tailed Lemurs:Wildlife World Zoo, AZ

Blue Macaws: Wildlife World Zoo, AZ

Broad-Billed Hummingbirds: AZ-Sonora Desert Museum

When photographing more than one subject, look at the behavior, position and pose of each subject. Try to catch them engaging in similar behavior, relating to one another or focusing attention in the same direction.

Start identifying animal behaviors: Are they eating, hunting, or playing? Are they showing fear or aggression? Are they stalking you? When there is more than one animal, how do they communicate with each other? How do they play together and take care of each other?

The key to getting an excellent photograph is to identify the cues that precede specific behaviors and to press halfway down the shutter button a second before the action starts.

For example:

* *A bird will defecate just before taking flight. Be ready to photograph the bird flying away.*

* *A cat will crouch down and get very focused on its target just before attacking. Be ready to photograph the cat leaping or running to its target.*

* *Water fowl will dunk their bodies into the water several times, and then stretch out and flap their wings. Be ready to photograph the bird when it lifts its body out of the water to flap its wings.*

Once you have a sense for anticipating animal behavior, then work on incorporating the other guidelines in this section.

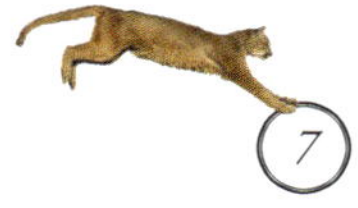

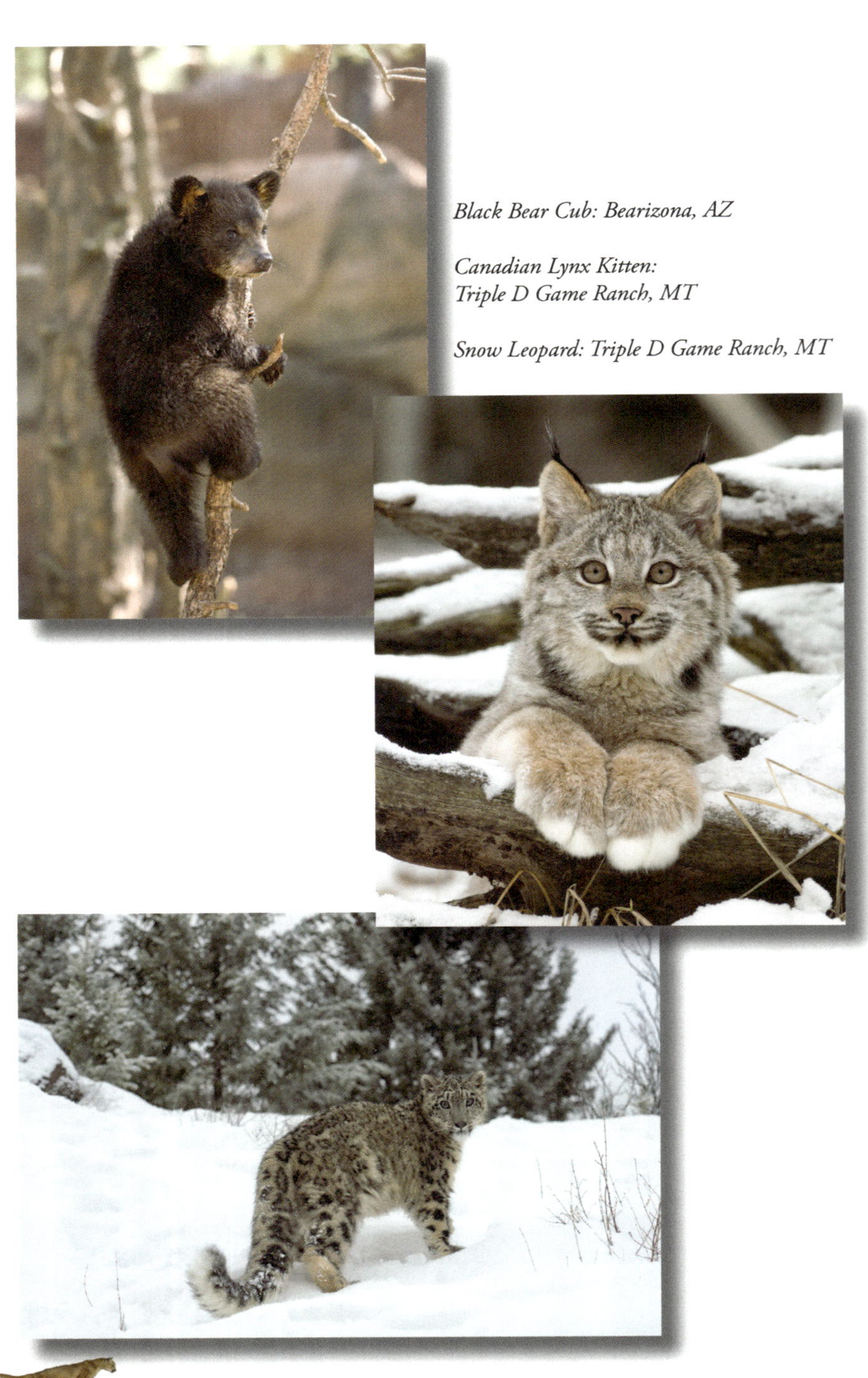

Black Bear Cub: Bearizona, AZ

Canadian Lynx Kitten:
Triple D Game Ranch, MT

Snow Leopard: Triple D Game Ranch, MT

3) Wait for a Pose

Ears facing forward will convey alertness and interest. A front leg slightly bent and lifted shows movement, and has more appeal, than when all limbs are outstretched. Legs should be distinct and separate (not over-lapping) in the photo to look natural. An animal glancing back at you over its shoulder creates an even more exciting dynamic.

Wait for an animal's tongue to be inside its mouth. A wolf with its tongue out loses its sense of mystery, looking instead like any other dog. If showing only a portion of an animal in the frame, avoid cropping at the joints (knees, ankles, elbows or knuckles).

4) Provide Room for the Subject to Move in the Frame

Give an animal space to move or look toward the center of the frame. An animal looking into the photo will help draw the viewer's eye into the photo. As a general rule, if the animal is looking up, place the animal near the bottom of the frame. If the animal is looking down, place it near the top of the frame. Recompose when the animal changes the direction it is looking or moving. Leave a bit of space around the edges; when subjects are too close to the borders in the frame, it appears awkward.

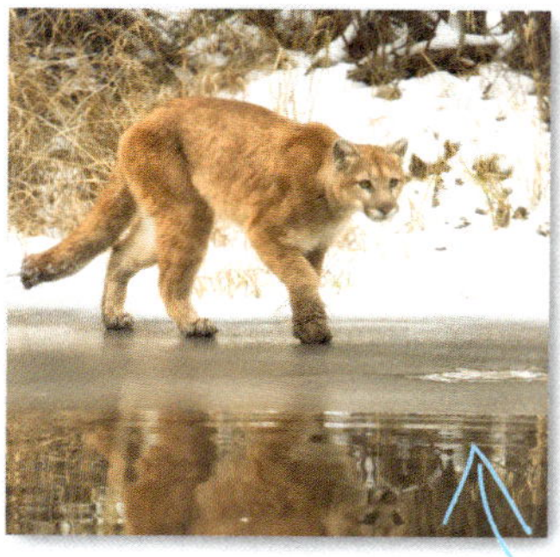

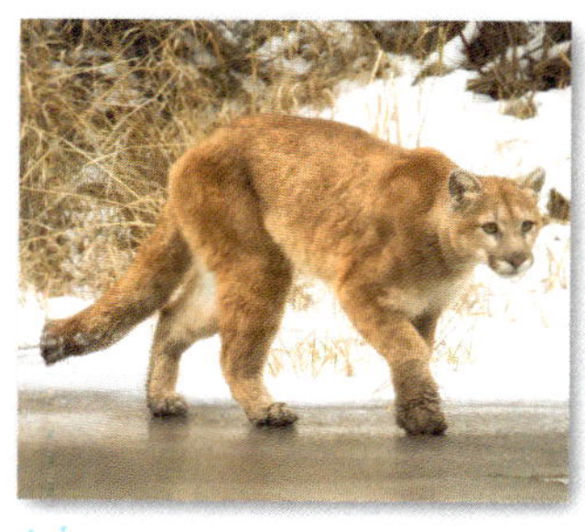

5) Keep Backgrounds Simple

To improve the composition of your wildlife photographs, you may want to include some of the animal's habitat or environment. Look at elements in the foreground and background that may enhance the photo. If the environment works, use it; but if unattractive, then zoom in for a tight close-up. Frame-filling detail is always intriguing.

Nothing should be sharper, brighter, more colorful, or in any way more attractive than the main subject.

Pay particular attention to what is behind the animal: A cluttered, distracting or ugly background can ruin an otherwise excellent composition. Look at the four corners and borders of your frame. Avoid objects that appear to be growing out of the top of your subject's head. Look for and eliminate hot spots (unattractive bright areas within the image).

Physically move your body left, right, up or down to eliminate distractions. Anything that does not improve the composition of the photo may make it worse.

When blurred, foliage makes a beautiful, uncluttered background. (See photo next page.) An out of focus background will draw the viewer's attention to the subject. To blur the background, use a telephoto lens with at least 200mm focal length, a wide aperture setting such as f/4, and be as physically close to the subject as possible.

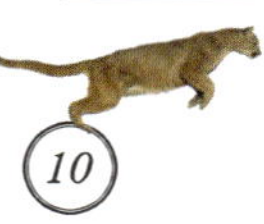

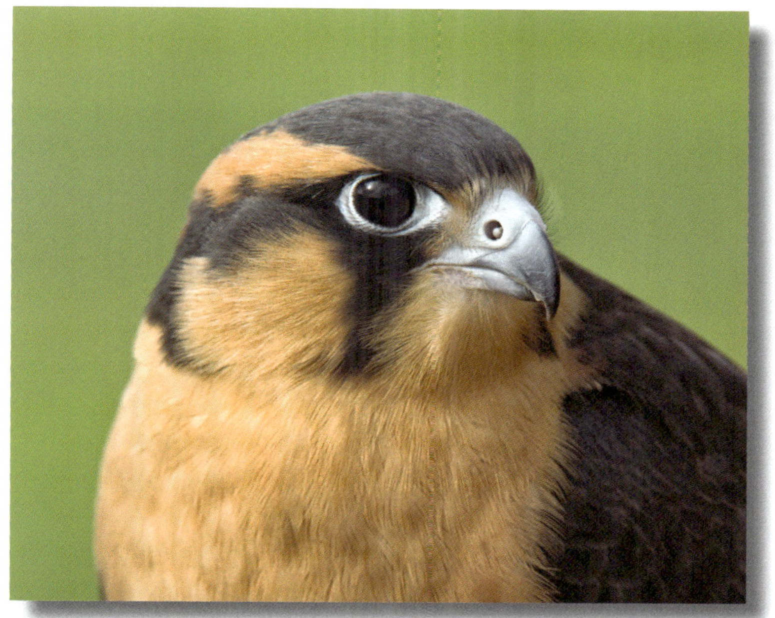

Aplomado Falcon: Teton Raptor Center, WY
Background is blurred foliage

Use the direction of movement, lines and curves in the frame (both obvious and implied) to draw the viewer's attention to the subject. Look for repetitive patterns and framing opportunities. Diagonal lines are more effective than horizontal or vertical because they create tension, movement and action.

Animals can create implied lines simply with their tail, their tracks, or with the direction they are looking or moving.

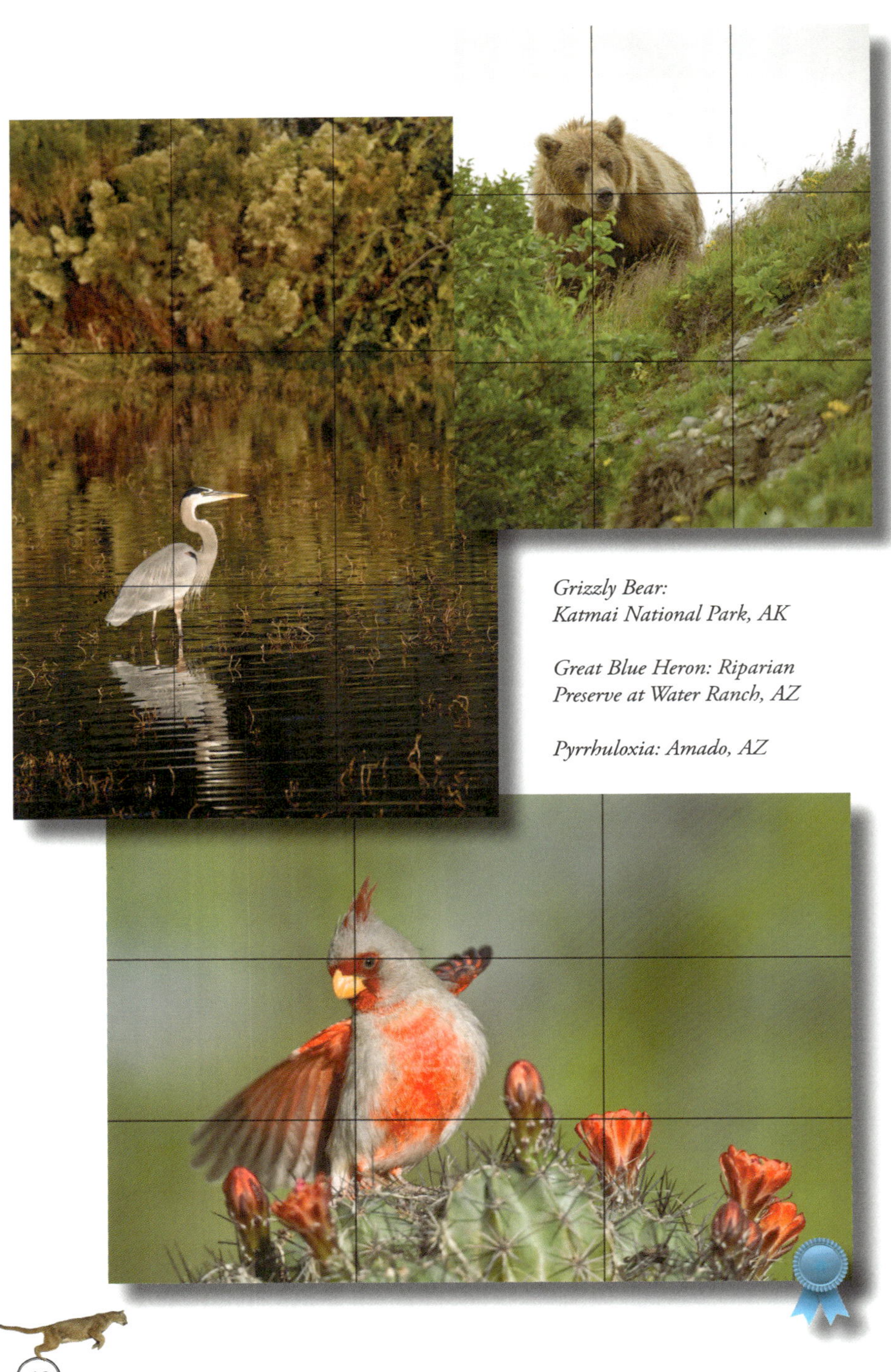

Grizzly Bear:
Katmai National Park, AK

Great Blue Heron: Riparian Preserve at Water Ranch, AZ

Pyrrhuloxia: Amado, AZ

6) Apply the Rule of Thirds

Inexperienced photographers tend to place their subject in the middle of the photo. To elevate your expertise, apply the "rule of thirds" when taking a photograph.

Deliberately place the subject or key focus point on one of the horizontal or vertical "third" lines, or at a point of intersection, to make the photo more interesting to the viewer.

To visualize the "rule of thirds" concept, look at the photo examples. Each photo has been divided into thirds horizontally and vertically, resulting in nine equally divided subdivisions.

According to the rule, a well-balanced, more dynamic photo is divided into thirds, and not in half. The four intersection points are "power points." By placing key features, such as the eyes, face or pose on a power point, the viewer's attention will immediately go to this point.

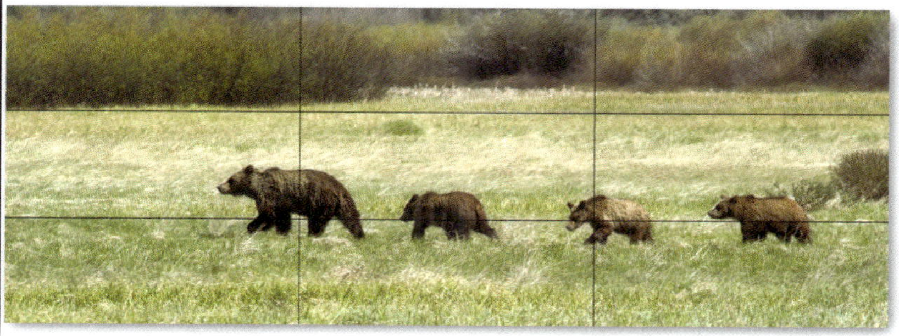

Grizzly Bears: Grand Teton National Park, WY

7) Photograph Wildlife in the Best Light

Use light to emphasize your subject, accentuate colors and create mood. Look where light illuminates the fur or body of an animal. As light reflects on a textured surface, it accentuates the look and feel.

Remember "light illuminates, shadows define."

Learn how to see highlights and shadows in a scene. Art is about the subtle differences between highlights and shadows and how they interact.

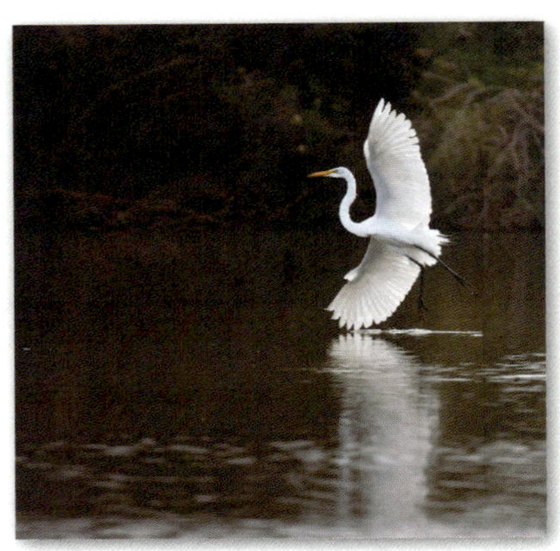

Great White Egret: Riparian Preserve at Water Ranch, AZ

Know whether you are seeing top light, front light, back light or side light, so that you can position yourself and wait for the animal to move into the most attractive spot within its environment.

Using front light in early morning or late afternoon is the best place to start training your eye to see light quality.

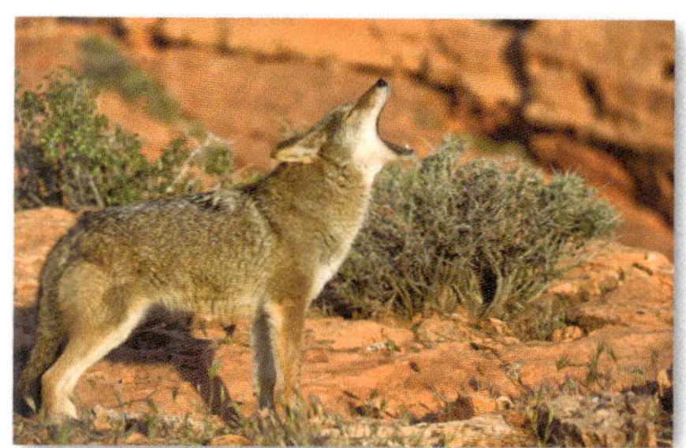

Side light captures texture and emphasizes the three dimensional qualities of the subject. A dark background will make a side lit subject even more dramatic.

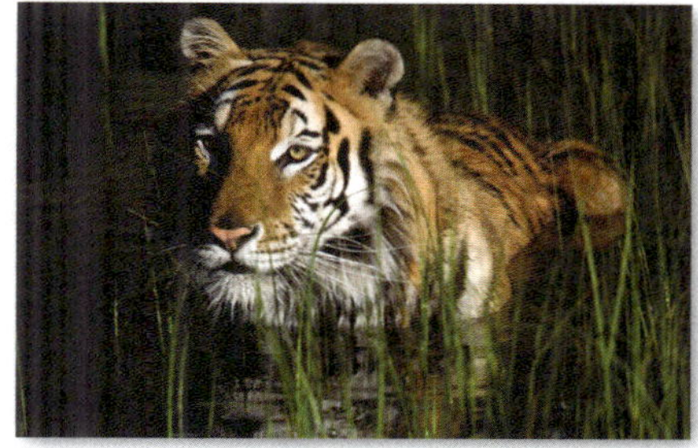

Back lighting is ideal for wildlife with shaggy fur or feathers. Use spot meter to expose the subject only (see the halo effect in photo to the right), or for a silhouetted effect, meter the background only.

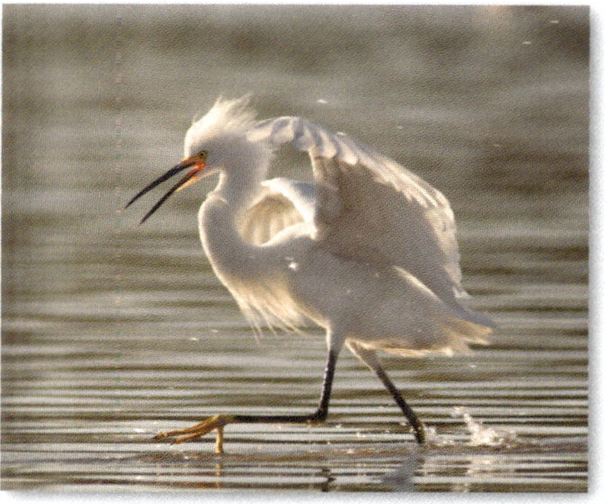

Mid-day light, if not used correctly, can be harsh and wash out colors. At this time of day, look for even light, all sun or all shade, to produce a good exposure.

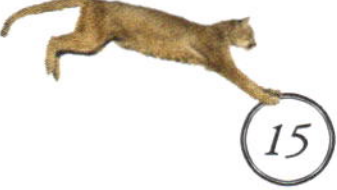

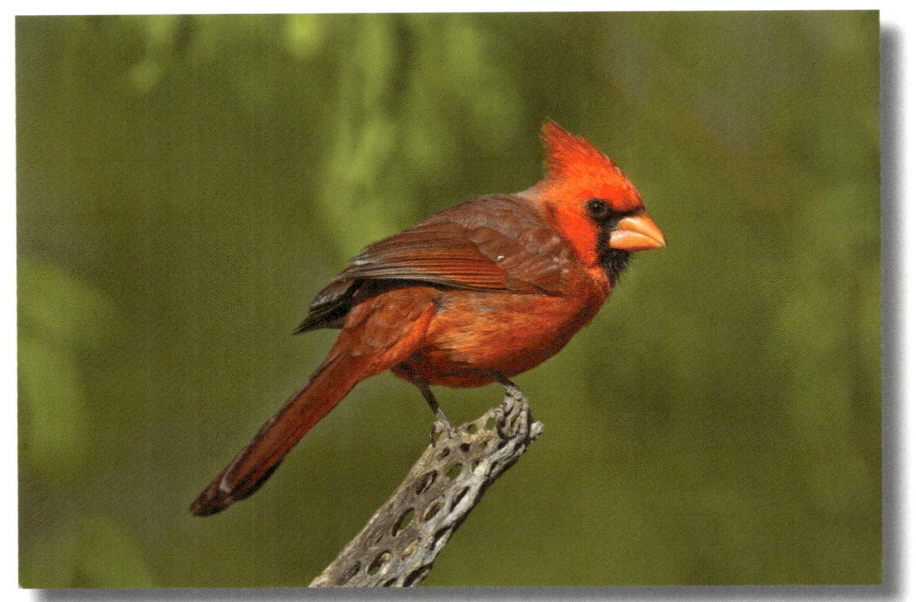

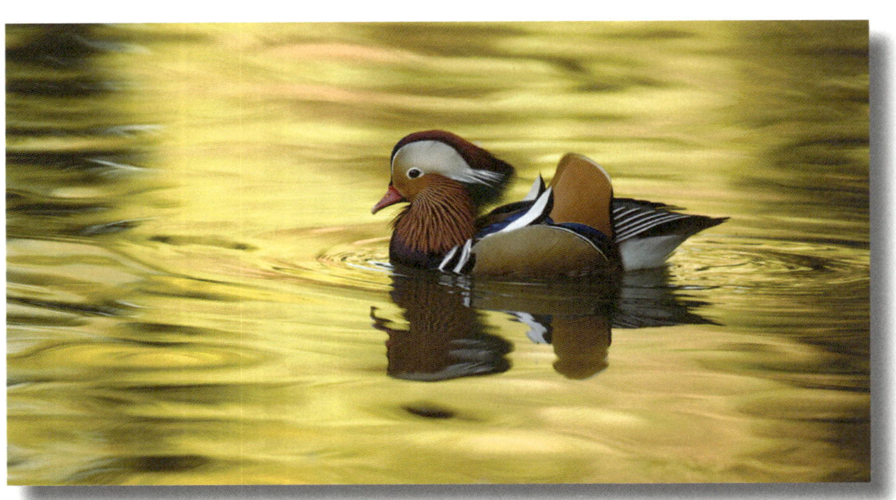

Northern Cardinal: Southern AZ
Mandarin Duck: Wildlife World Zoo, AZ

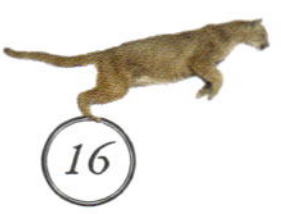

8) Use Color for Impact

Color evokes the greatest emotional reaction. The color red for example has the most visual power, because it represents excitement, fire, food, warmth and danger.

Look for opportunities to add color to your photos:

* *Warm colors have more impact than cool colors.*

* *Colors are more impactful when they are not diluted by white or black.*

* *Colors gain strength when combined with an opposite or complementary color.*

9) Respect Their World

Be respectful and considerate of animals. Do not clap, whistle, shout or throw things. Never attempt to feed or touch a wild animal, and never turn your back on a wild animal.

Never interfere with animals' movements, habitat or natural behavior in order to take a better photo. Watch their body language. *Have they noticed you? Do they feel threatened? Have they become agitated? Do they consider you prey?*

If you hear something, stop and listen, as they would. Approach slowly and do not make sudden moves. Stop regularly and once you find a good position, stay still. Be careful not to act like a predator. It is actually better to be stationary and let wildlife approach you.

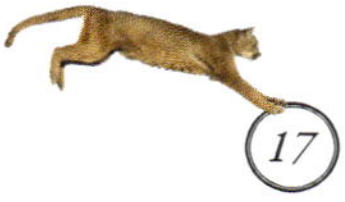

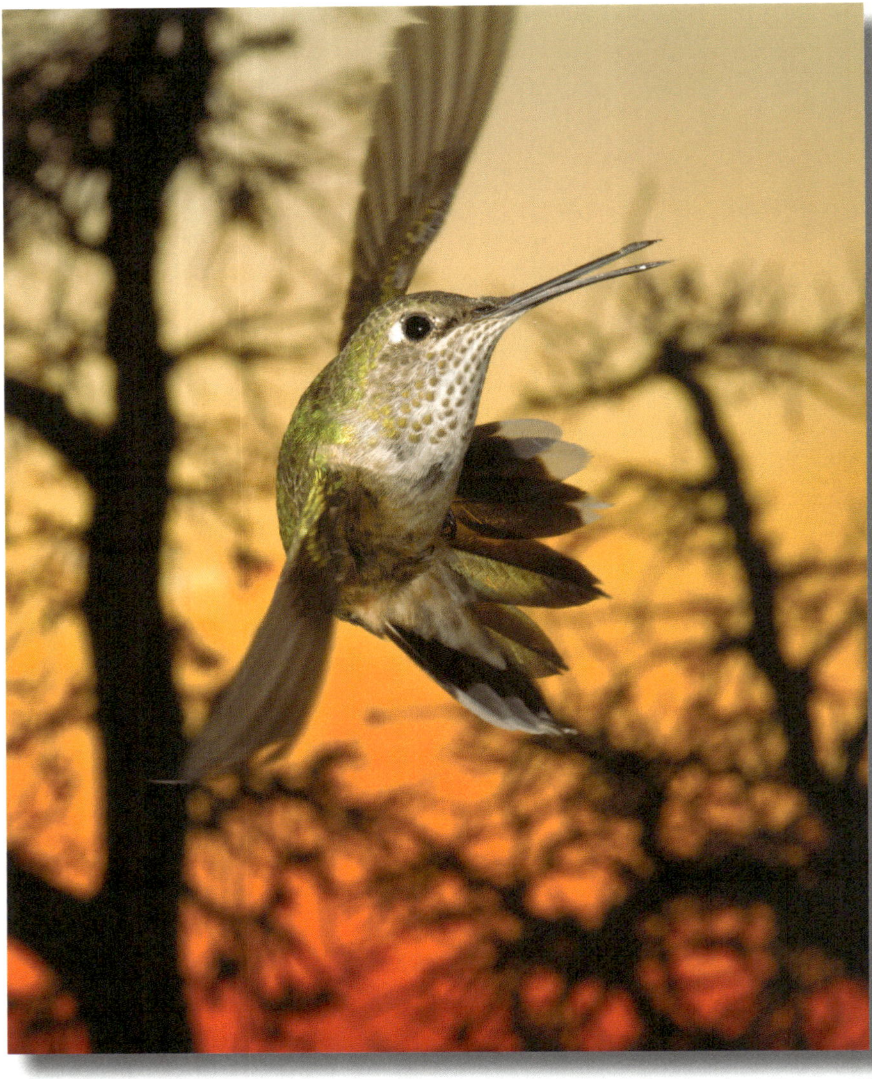

Broad-Tailed Hummingbird: Payson, AZ

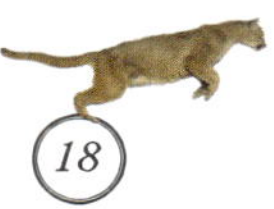

Preparing to Photograph Wildlife

Being prepared makes the experience even more enjoyable. This section outlines what you should be familiar with before you arrive at your photography location:

1) Practicing with Different Camera Functions
2) Choosing a Lens
3) Mastering Electronic Flash
4) Researching the Location and Wildlife
5) Anticipating Optimal Light
6) Bringing the Essential Equipment
7) Wearing Appropriate Clothing
8) Packing the Night Before

1) Practicing with Different Camera Functions

Knowing how to operate your equipment *before you are on location* increases your odds of getting a fantastic photograph. The more you experiment with different camera functions, the more possibilities you will have for creative control.

Practice at home and around your neighborhood. There is usually wildlife close by and if not, a pet can serve as an excellent and [sometimes] accommodating subject. When you go outside for a walk, or go for a drive, take your camera. Do you have a birdfeeder? Set one up or drop a few bird seeds on a rock or fence post to attract birds. There are lots of opportunities to practice before you travel.

In the charts that follow, you will find the camera functions used most frequently for wildlife photography. Practice these functions with your camera. For additional details, read your camera manual.

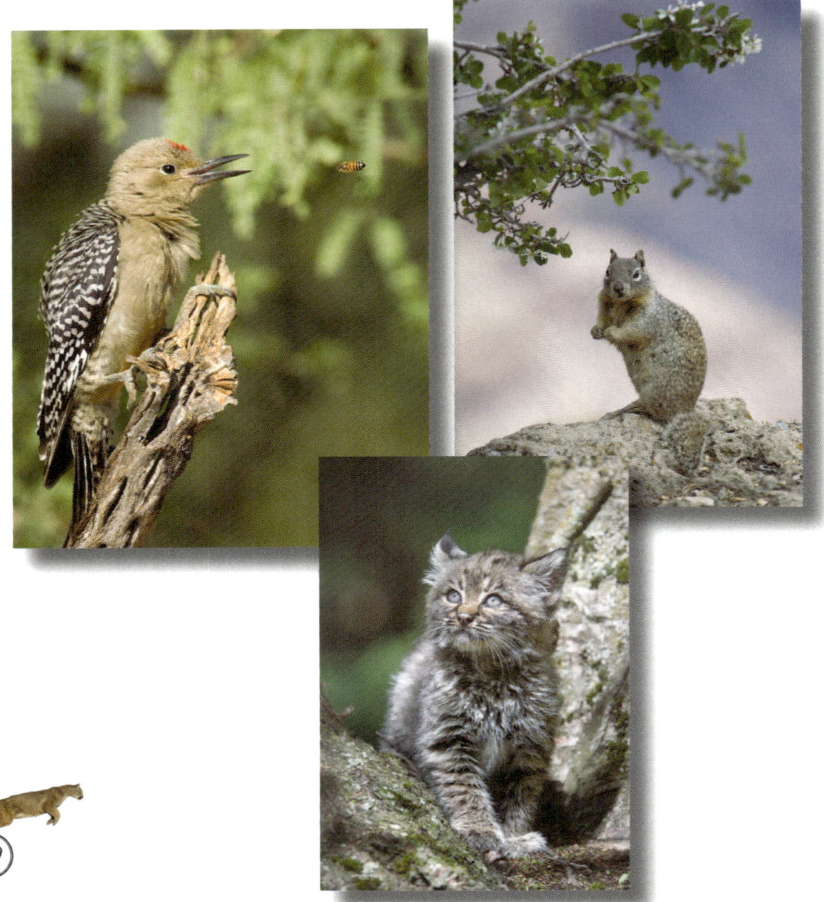

CAMERA FUNCTIONS Function	Purpose	What to Know
Exposure Mode	Determines how the camera sets shutter speed and aperture when adjusting exposure	How to switch between Aperture Priority, Shutter Priority, and Manual Mode
ISO Sensitivity	Enables higher shutter speeds and/or smaller apertures for a correct exposure	How to switch from Auto Mode to a particular ISO setting How to increase/decrease ISO How high the ISO can be set before digital noise and/or color distortion is noticeable
Aperture	Controls amount of light through the lens and how much of the photo is in sharp focus	How to adjust the aperture f-stop in Manual Mode or Aperture Priority Mode
Shutter Speed	Controls the amount of time light is let in by the camera Used to freeze or blur motion	How to adjust the shutter speed in Manual Mode or Shutter Speed Priority Mode
Metering Mode	Controls how much of the photo frame is used by the camera to calculate exposure	How to switch between Evaluative (aka Matrix), Center-Weighted, and Spot Metering to control exposure
White Balance	Defines the light source in order to make white objects appear white in photos	How to switch White Balance from Auto Mode to a setting such as Sunny or Cloudy
Focus Mode	Enables auto focus or manual focus (Auto focus determines whether the camera focuses once or continuously when the shutter is pressed halfway)	How to switch Focus Mode between Continuous Servo (aka AI Servo) and Single Servo (aka One-Shot AF)

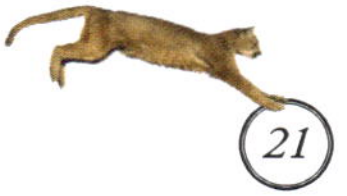

CAMERA FUNCTIONS

Function	Purpose	What to Know
Auto Focus Area Mode	Determines area of the frame the camera will use to focus	How to select and adjust the Auto Focus point(s)
Drive Mode	Determines the number of photos the camera takes when the shutter is pressed	How to switch between Single, Low-Speed Continuous, and High-Speed Continuous
Depth of Field Preview	Previews the effects of the selected aperture *With smaller apertures such as* f/18 *the photo will appear darker through the viewfinder; but will show the sharpness achieved*	Where the preview button is on the camera
Exposure Compensation	Enables an increase or decrease in image exposure	How to alter exposure from a value suggested by the camera to make photos brighter or darker
Histogram	Displays a graphic representation of the range of tones from dark to light in a photo	How to display and read a histogram
Blinkies	Displays where the photo is overexposed (too much light)	How to show highlights
Playback Zoom	Zooms in on the image displayed on the LCD	How to zoom to 100% to confirm the desired sharpness
Image Area	Defines the size of the image sensor	How to switch between FX and DX format (if available)
Image Quality	Controls the file format and quantity of data in the resulting image	How to switch between JPEG and RAW image quality

2) Choosing a Lens

When it comes to lenses, start with the best quality glass within your budget. Next, pick a focal length that will be best for the subjects you want to photograph. Focal length, in the simplest of terms, determines how far away you will be able to photograph a subject. The table below lists my lenses and how I typically use them to photograph wildlife.

LENSES Focal Length Maximum Aperture	Minimum Focus Distance	Wildlife Uses
60mm macro **f/2.8**	.72 feet	Close up: Small mammals/reptiles Aquariums
105mm macro **f/2.8**	1 foot	Close up: Small mammals/reptiles Butterflies/insects Small mammal portraits
180mm macro f/3.5 **200mm macro f/4**	1.5 feet 1.6 feet	Close up: Hummingbirds
24-70mm **f/2.8**	1.3 feet	Groups/packs close range Medium mammal portraits
70-200mm VRII **f/2.8**	4.6 feet	Raptors in flight Large mammals Groups/packs
200-400mm VRII f/4	6.6 feet	Medium/Large mammals Large mammal/raptor portraits
150-500mm **f/5-6.3**	7.2 feet	Large mammal portraits Medium mammals behind a fence Large mammals behind a fence
600mm **f/4**	15.7 feet	Small birds from a blind Large mammals behind a fence Large birds in flight

3) Mastering Electronic Flash

Electronic flash is either a built-in flash (commonly called pop-up flash) that is physically part of the camera, or an external flash unit that connects into the camera shoe which is on top of the camera.

Artificial light can be used as the only light source, or to supplement natural light.

The goal with flash is to add only enough light to get the desired effect, and no more.

At a minimum, understand how to use the flash functions noted in the table below.

FLASH FUNCTIONS

Function	Purpose	Essential to Know
Flash Mode	Determines the flash output	How to switch between TTL (Through the Lens) and Manual mode
Flash Synch Speed	Determines the shutter speed needed to achieve proper flash exposure	How to synchronize the camera shutter speed with the flash
Flash Output Level Compensation	Enables an increase or decrease in flash output	How to alter the flash output to make the main subject brighter or darker

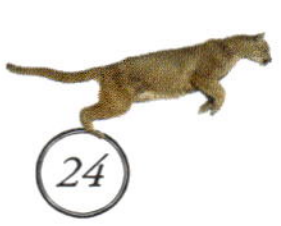

4) Researching the Location and Wildlife

Are you going to a park, preserve, wildlife refuge, nature reserve or zoo? Will you be driving through, walking or hiking? Is it a short or long journey? Whatever the choice, research and familiarize yourself with the area and wildlife.

a. Research the topography including: mountains, hills, creeks, meadows, orchards, ponds/lakes, and their elevation. Pay particular attention to the level of physical energy required to reach your location and return home safely. Obtain applicable maps.

b. Look up average temperatures including the highs and lows, and average precipitation including rain and snow. Identify any other climate conditions and seasonal changes that impact habitats and seasonal wildlife migrations.

c. Study the indigenous wildlife, including threatened and recovering species. Pay particular attention to knowing what wildlife could be dangerous, such as poisonous snakes. Even if you are going to a zoo, there will still be some indigenous wildlife nearby. Sometimes photographers get in trouble with wildlife because they just do not know any better. Keep yourself safe by doing your homework.

d. Think about wildlife in terms of their needs. Animals are concerned with their safety and food. They are either prey or predator. Each species has a different "threat zone."

e. Consider guides, tours and photo workshops in wildlife areas; increase your opportunities to capture some incredible photographs. At a minimum, talk to other photographers who have been there and look at photos taken at the location.

f. Identify wildlife park hours, fees and required permits.

Wildlife parks and zoos are a great place to practice observing animal behaviors and mastering your camera functions in preparation for a longer wildlife trip.

Here are additional tips for wildlife parks and zoos:

* **Join as a member.** You will not need to pay every time you visit; therefore, you will not mind being at the park only in the early morning and late afternoon (for the best light). Plus, you will be contributing to the care of the wildlife. *(A healthy, happy animal makes for a more pleasing photograph!)*
* **You may get early access.** Some parks let members enter earlier than the public.
* **Talk to the park or zoo staff.** Caregivers and docents are knowledgeable about the animals and enjoy sharing their knowledge.
* **Plan to go as a photographer,** not as a tourist. Go alone to minimize distractions. Give yourself plenty of time.
* **Plan to go mid-week** when the park or zoo is less crowded. In addition, try to avoid holidays.

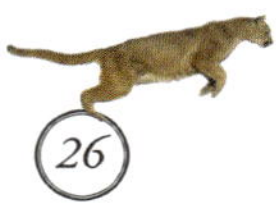

5) Anticipating Optimal Light

Professional photographers see the subject and the light; and therefore, plan for when the light will be best for the desired composition.

a. Look up the time of sunrise/sunset. Typically, you should plan to arrive 30 minutes before sunrise and leave about 30 minutes after sunset.

b. Whenever possible, photograph in the early morning or late afternoon, because the light is warmer and the angle of light creates long shadows, depth and texture. The sun will catch the full face of the subject and produce a beautiful catch light in the animal's eyes. Wildlife tends to venture into the open just before dawn and just after dusk. This time of day is referred to as "golden hour" or "magic light."

c. Avoid midday light when the sun is high overhead. Mid-day light creates high contrast between the bright highlights and dark shadows. As a result, the colors and texture of an animal appear washed out. An animal's eyes can be lost in the shadow of massive brows during the midday hours. In addition, animals often sleep during the heat of the day, which minimizes opportunities.

d. Photograph on a lightly overcast day; it provides even, non-directional light. Referred to as "soft light," this setting can help to enhance the richness of the color tones and texture of an animal.

e. Do not cancel your plans because storms are brooding or passing over; storms stir excitement in wildlife.

6) Bringing the Essential Equipment

The photography equipment you bring will depend on the location, the length of your stay, and the wildlife you plan to photograph. Use the following list as a checklist for determining what to bring.

Insure all of your equipment!

Equipment Description	Considerations
Camera Bodies	1 or 2 camera bodies Fully charged batteries Extra batteries Battery charger Manuals
Lenses	Super telephoto (300-600mm) Telephoto zoom (70-300mm) Wide angle (24-70mm) Macro (60 – 100mm) Teleconverter: to extend the focal length of your lens Extension Tubes: to reduce the minimum focus distance Manuals
Flash & Lighting Accessories	Off camera flash unit Extra batteries Flash manual Diffuser(s)/soft boxes Remote cord to use the flash off-camera Battery charger
Tripod, Monopod & Heads	Tripod (must withstand 30% more than your heaviest camera/lens) Monopod Ball head or gimbal head on the tripod and monopod

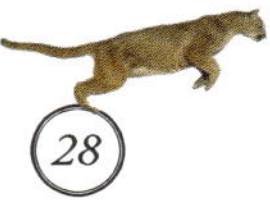

Equipment Description	Considerations
Camera Bags Packs & Cases	A backpack
Memory Cards	High Capacity Cards (i.e., 32 gigabyte cards)
Filters	UV Polarizer Graduated Neutral Density
Laptop Computer & Storage Devices	Backup Storage Device
Miscellaneous Equipment	Lens dust remover and cleaning supplies Remote shutter release Flashlight Binoculars Map Sunscreen/bug repellent Large plastic garbage bag to sit on or use in case of rain Knee pads Small note pad and pens Cell phone

7) **Wearing Appropriate Clothing**

a. Dress for the weather (layers are always best). Remember it is cooler in the mornings and in the late afternoons. When you need gloves, wear ones that will still allow you to work the controls on your camera.

b. Wear closed-toe, comfortable walking shoes/hiking boots.

c. Wear colors that blend into your surroundings. For example, in the desert, wear tan and beige.

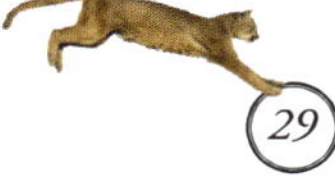

d. Wear high-SPF sunscreen on your face and neck to avoid getting sunburn during a long day. Even in warm weather, cover your skin with light weight clothing.

e. Consider a camera vest with pockets or a belt pack that is turned around to be in front of you; you will be less likely to set down any equipment and walk away from it.

f. Wear a wide brim hat to protect your neck from getting sunburned and keep your eyes shaded.

g. Avoid wearing perfume or strong scents. Remember, even clothes detergent and bug spray can have a strong scent.

h. When there is any chance of rain, be prepared to keep you and your gear dry.

8) Packing the Night Before

a. Select the camera settings that you are most likely to use.

b. Check that all equipment is functioning properly, especially rented equipment.

c. Charge all camera and flash batteries.

Don't forget to pack this book and a pen for notes. ;)

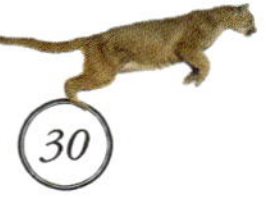

d. Download all photos from your memory cards, and then reformat all memory cards. Do this before leaving for location. Reformatting does not mean to simply delete old photos; it means to completely clean off all visible and invisible data on the memory card. This is critical for ensuring that memory cards do not fail with use over time. Reformat cards in the camera rather than on the computer to ensure they are formatted according to your camera's specifications.

e. Clean your camera sensor regularly. Some cameras have an automatic sensor cleaner function. Local camera stores offer a cleaning service for a fee. Alternatively, you can clean it yourself if you have thoroughly read and understand how to do it from the instructions in your manual. Be forewarned, it is not easy to do!

f. Clean the CPU contacts on your camera and lenses with a cotton swab to remove dust (no alcohol/solution is needed). Be sure the camera is turned off when removing your lens.

g. Clean the lens glass. To remove dirt and smudges from your lens, use a blower brush and/or a micro-fiber cleaning cloth and lens cleaner. (Never put liquid cleaner directly on the lens; put cleaner on the cloth.)

h. Pack your camera bag to be sure everything you need is included and fits.

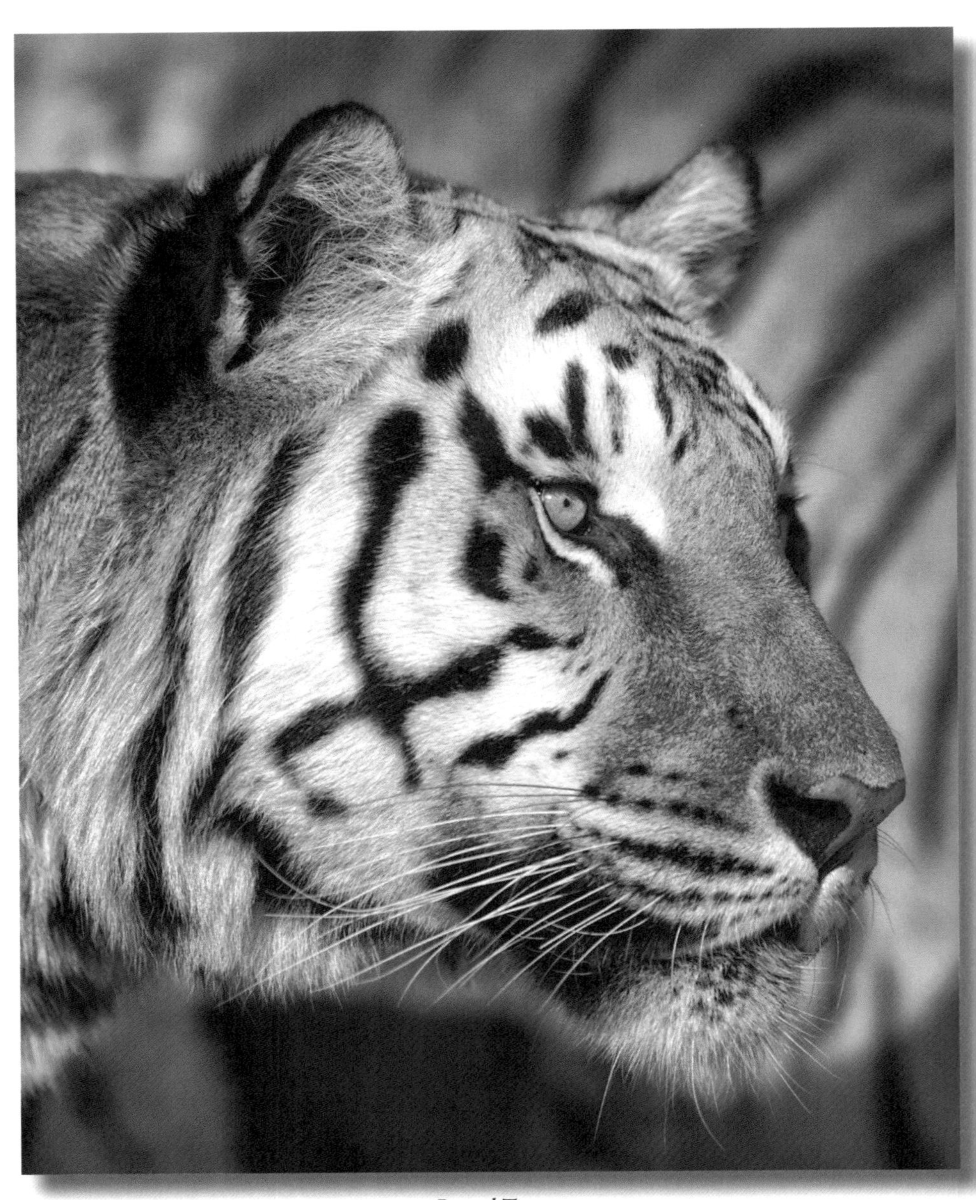

Bengal Tiger:
Out of Africa Wildlife Park, Camp Verde, AZ

SECTION 3

Picking the Optimal Camera Settings

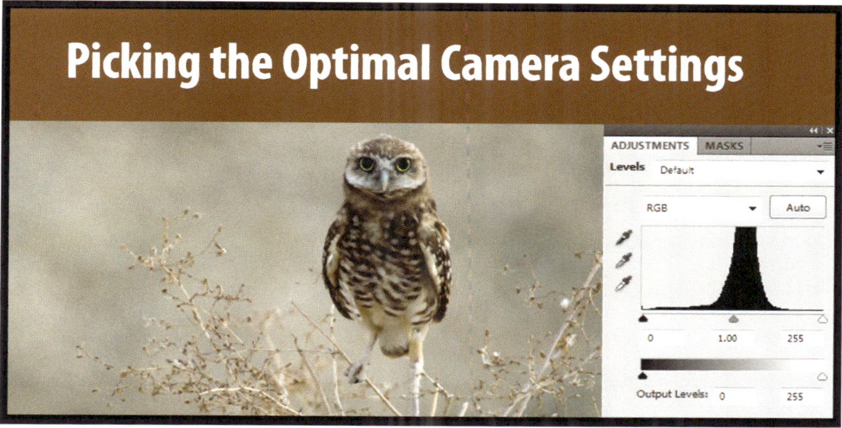

A number of variables need to be considered when selecting camera settings. This section outlines the important considerations and suggested settings for wildlife photography. Suggested settings in this section are highlighted.

Have your camera next to you as you read this section and practice making the suggested adjustments as you read along. For some of you, this section may be a review; for others who have never changed settings from Auto, this may seem a bit daunting at first. Hang in there, I promise this will get easier the more you practice.

This section will highlight the following key settings:

1) Image Quality
2) Exposure Mode
3) ISO Sensitivity
4) Metering Mode
5) White Balance
6) Exposure Compensation
7) Auto Focus Settings

1) Image Quality

Most cameras offer several image quality formats, and some offer the ability to record images in multiple formats simultaneously. For most photographers today, RAW format is the format of choice, but there are good reasons to use JPEG in certain situations.

RAW Format

The camera records what it sees without processing the image. A post-processing software program is needed to interpret and process the image.

RAW gives you a great deal of flexibility and control in processing your images to get the most from your subject, but it requires more work and more storage space, and slows down the camera.

JPEG Format

The camera records the image and applies the in-camera pre-selected settings to produce a quick finished product. JPEG offers less flexibility and control, but requires less work and storage space.

2) Exposure Mode

The Exposure Mode function allows you to choose the degree to which you want to control aperture and shutter speed. *The aperture is critical to the appearance of your image, as it is one of the controlling factors in determining how much of the image is in focus.*

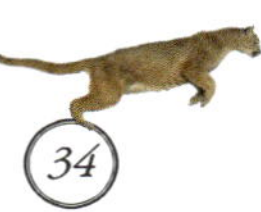

Mode	Description	When to Use	Examples
APERTURE PRIORITY (A or AV) Mode	You set aperture and the camera sets shutter speed	For animal portraits To soften or blur the background, use a large aperture (which is a small f-stop number) To make the fence disappear when photographing a stationary animal through a fence (Requires at least 200mm lens focal length)	*One animal:* f/2.8 – f/6.3 *Two plus animals:* f/8 – F/11

The longer the focal length of the lens (i.e., 400 mm) and the closer you are to the subject, the easier it is to blur the background by using a large aperture setting.

Aperture Priority Mode Examples

In the following photos, take note of the settings and the effect they have on the image.

Gray Wolf
Aperture: f/4
Shutter Speed: 1/1600s
ISO: 500
Lens Focal Length: 400mm

Effect: shallow depth of field, eyes in sharp focus

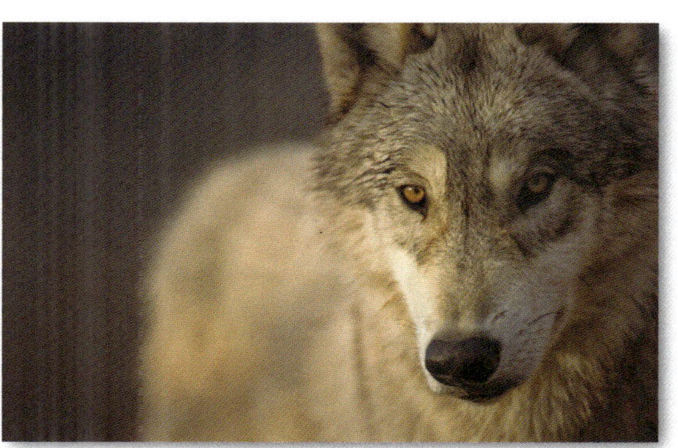

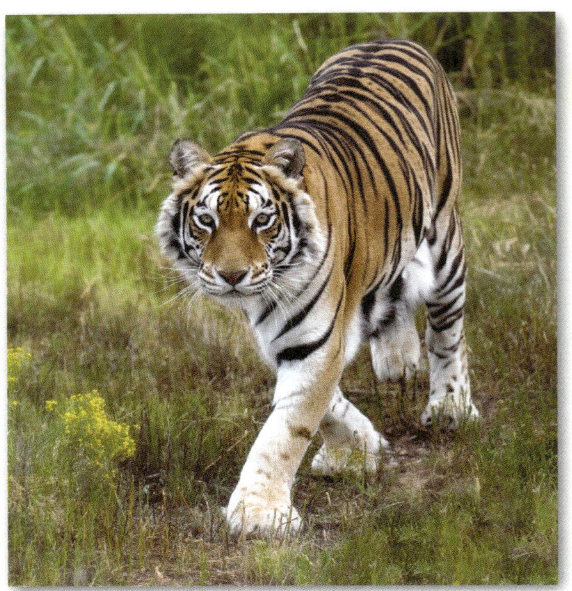

Bengal Tiger
Aperture: f/4.5
Shutter Speed: 1/400s
ISO: 400
Lens Focal Length: 200mm

Effect: Face in sharp focus, background softened

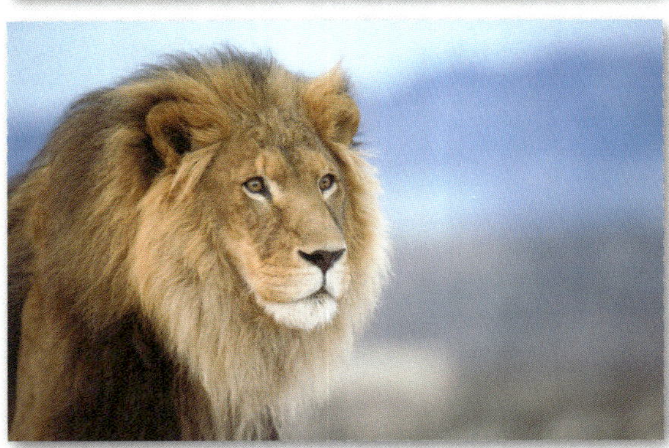

African Lion
Aperture: f/4
Shutter Speed: 1/500s
ISO: 5000
Lens Focal Length: 400mm

Effect: High ISO for low light conditions, distracting background blurred

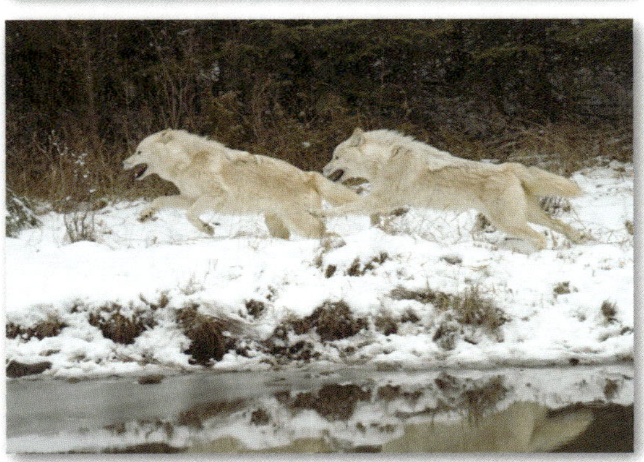

Arctic Wolves
Aperture: f/10
Shutter Speed: 1/640s
ISO: 2500
Lens Focal Length: 120mm

Effect: Higher f-stop for sharp focus, high ISO to ensure sufficient shutter speed

Mode	Description	When to Use	Examples
SHUTTER PRIORITY (S or TV) Mode	You set shutter speed and the camera chooses aperture	To freeze the action of a fast moving animal (Use a fast shutter which is a fraction of a second)	*Mammals running:* 1/500s – 1/1000s *Fast moving animals:* 1/1000s +
		To photograph birds flying	*Birds flying in natural light:* 1/2000s +
		To use flash for adding light	*Small animals through Plexiglas using single flash:* 1/200s - 1/250s

To ensure a sharp photo when hand-holding your camera, the shutter speed should not go below the focal length of your lens (and never below 1/60s). For example, when handholding a 70-200mm lens, shutter speed should not go below 1/200s.

Shutter Priority Mode Examples

In the following photos, take note of the settings and the effect they have on the image.

Grizzly Bear
Aperture: f/7
Shutter Speed: 1/1000s
ISO: 1250
Lens Focal Length: 400mm

Effect: High shutter speed to freeze motion, higher ISO for low light conditions

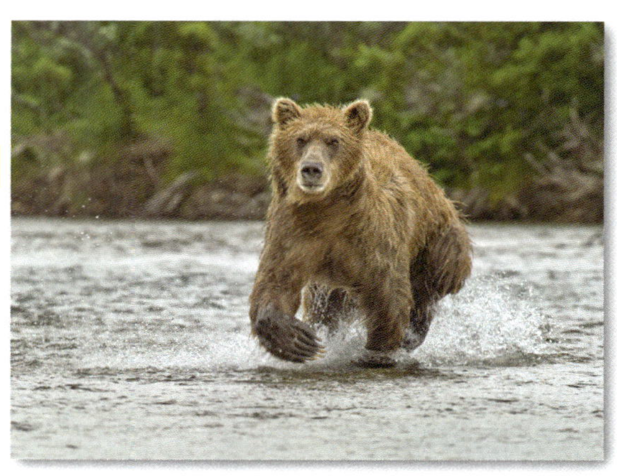

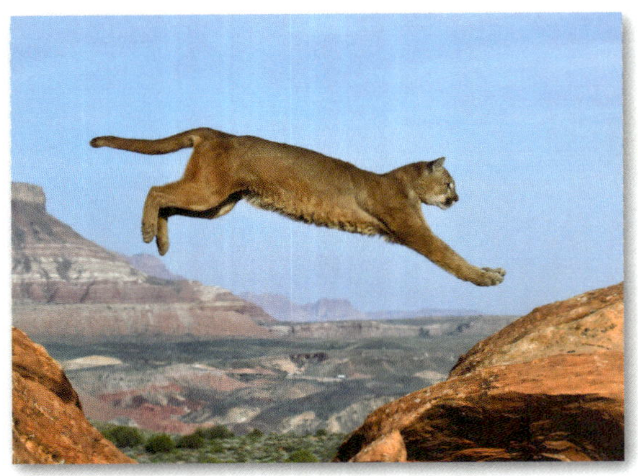

Mountain Lion
Aperture: f/8
Shutter Speed: 1/3200s
ISO: 1600
Lens Focal Length: 82mm

Effect: Extremely high shutter speed to freeze motion

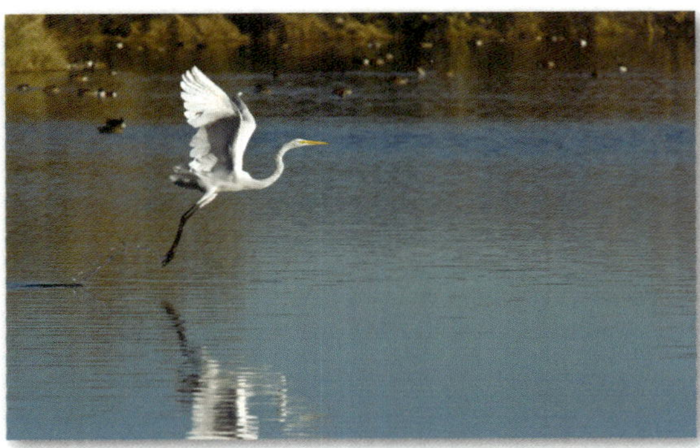

Great White Egret
Aperture: f/16
Shutter Speed: 1/2500s
ISO: 2000
Lens Focal Length: 490mm

Effect: Extremely high shutter speed to freeze motion, high f-stop to increase depth of field

Mode	Description	When to Use	Examples
MANUAL (M) Mode	You set aperture and shutter speed	To photograph a fast moving animal through a fence To use one or more flash To have complete control of shutter speed and depth of field	*Fast moving animal through a fence:* f/4 – 6.3 1/500s – 1/1000s *Hummingbirds flying, using multiple flash:* f/18 1/200s - 1/250s *Butterflies, using single flash:* f/18 1/200 - 1/250s

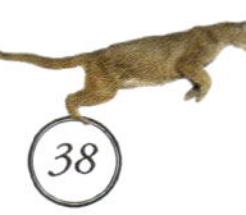

Manual Priority Mode Examples

In the following photos, take note of the settings and the effect they have on the image.

Osprey in Flight
Aperture: f/6.3
Shutter Speed: 1/2000s
ISO: 2000
Lens Focal Length: 1000mm

Effect: Small f-stop to blur background, high shutter speed to freeze motion

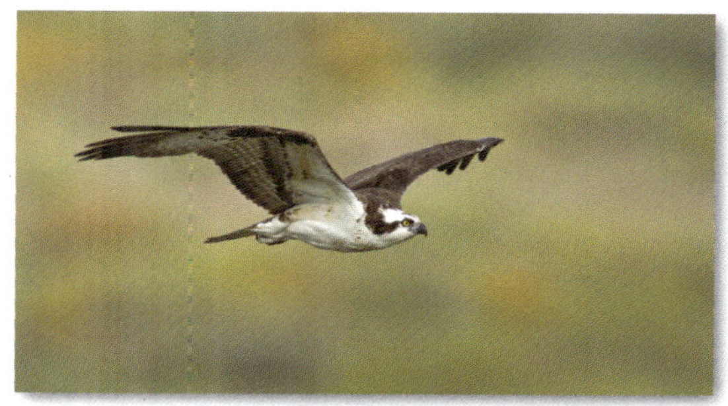

Black Bear Cub
Aperture: f/8
Shutter Speed: 1/1250s
ISO: 2800
Lens Focal Length: 280mm

Effect: Medium f-stop to ensure face in sharp focus, high shutter speed to freeze motion

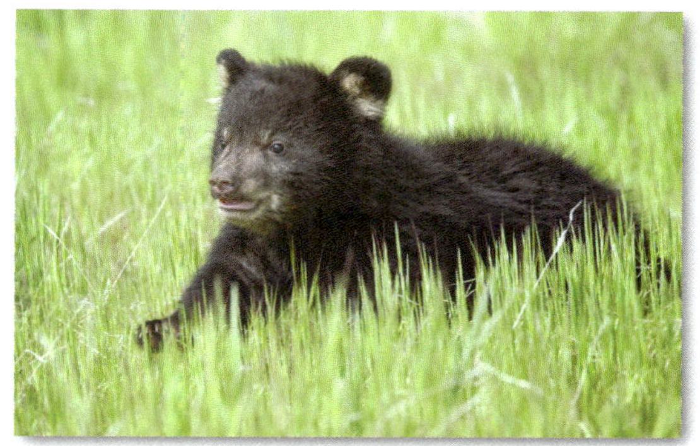

Juvenile Hummingbird in Natural Light
Aperture: f/5
Shutter Speed: 1/800s
ISO: 1250
Lens Focal Length: 180mm

Effect: Small f-stop to blur distracting background, relatively high shutter speed to freeze body motion

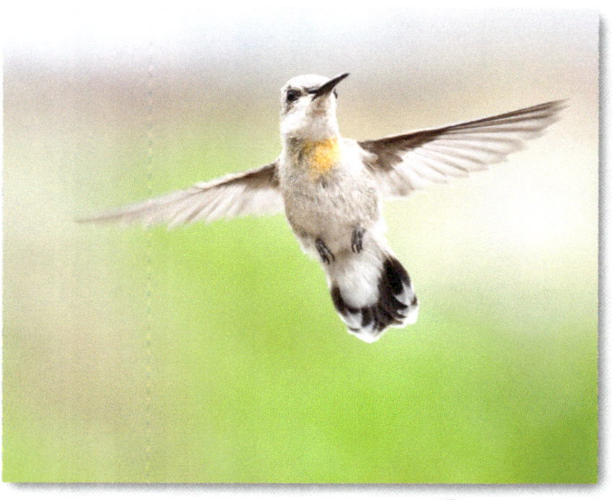

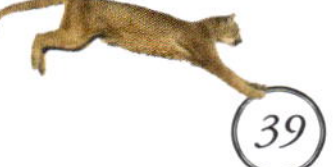

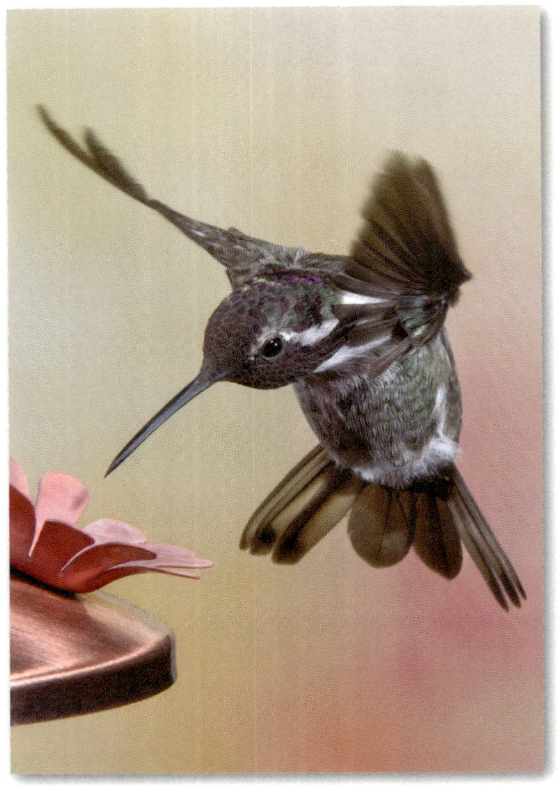

Hummingbird
Using multiple flash
Aperture: f/22
Shutter Speed: 1/250s
ISO: 200
Lens Focal Length: 400mm

Effect: High f-stop for extreme depth of field, flash freezes motion

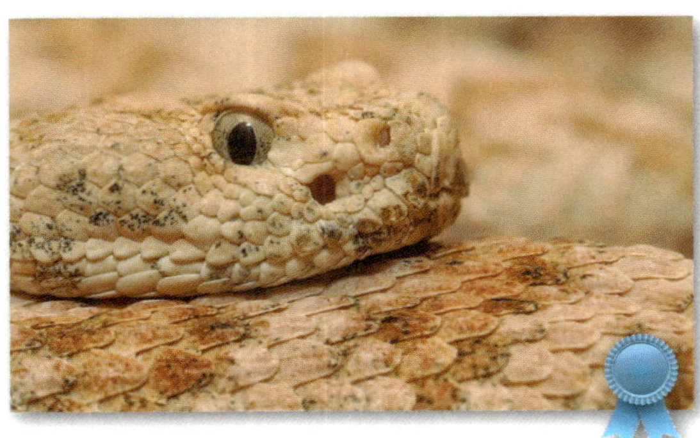

Speckled Rattlesnake
Through Plexiglas®
Using single flash
Aperture: f/16
Shutter Speed: 1/250s
ISO: 200
Lens Focal Length: 105mm macro

Effect: High f-stop for reasonable depth of field using macro lens

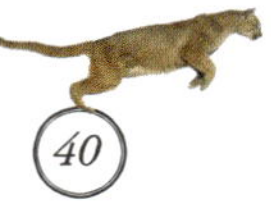

Mode	Description	When to Use
PROGRAM (P) Mode	Programs designed for common subject types: You choose the subject and the camera sets aperture/shutter speed	*Programs commonly used for wildlife* Actions/Sports (sometimes displayed as a skier icon): Use for fast moving wildlife to freeze the movement Portrait (sometimes displayed as a woman with a hat on): Use for animal portraits to throw the background out of focus
AUTO Mode	Camera sets everything	When you are unsure of what else to use or someone else uses your camera

3) ISO Sensitivity

ISO indicates the amount of light necessary to give a proper exposure. ISO sensitivity is the digital equivalent of film speed, represented as a numerical value, such as ISO 100. The higher the ISO value, the less light that is needed to make an exposure. A higher ISO allows higher shutter speeds or lower apertures (higher f-stop values). However, the higher the ISO, the more digital noise (equivalent to a grainy look in a film photo) will be visible; there is always a trade-off.

The general rule is to use the lowest ISO possible in order to obtain the intended result. For wildlife photography, ISO 800 is a great default ISO setting. Review the photos in Section 2 and notice the varying ISO settings. Sometimes it is necessary to increase ISO in order to achieve the shutter speed required for the subject.

4) Metering Mode

Exposure meters are designed to calculate an exposure reading of 18% gray, or perceptually about halfway between white and black. The selected metering mode tells the camera which parts of the frame to use in calculating exposure.

Cameras have different modes for calculating a correct exposure, for example:

NIKON®	CANON®
Matrix	Evaluative
	Partial
Spot	Spot
Center-weighted	Center-weighted Average

Matrix Metering or Evaluative Metering

This is the default mode for your camera. The camera meters a large portion of the entire frame and sets the exposure based on brightness, color, distance and composition to render a natural result. Use Matrix or Evaluative Metering Mode for most of your wildlife photography work.

On some cameras, this mode is required to do active tracking of the subject through the frame, which is very useful when photographing mammals running.

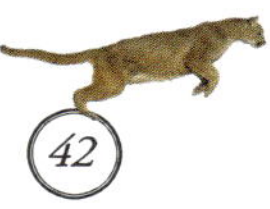

Center-Weighted Metering

The camera meters the entire frame, but assigns the greatest weight to the center area of the viewfinder. Center-weighted metering has limited use for wildlife photography because the subject is ideally not in the center of the frame.

Spot Metering

The camera meters a small circle in the frame. The circle is centered on the current focus point, which can be moved around within the frame. Use spot metering mode when your subject is significantly brighter or darker than the rest of your scene, and you want exposure to be perfect for the subject (not caring as much about the rest of the scene's exposure). Put the focus point directly on your subject, and your subject will be properly exposed.

An example of spot metering is shown below. The leopard was sleeping in bright mid-day sun, and was surrounded by shade.

By spot metering on the brightest part of the leopard, the exposure was correct for the leopard and the shady parts of the frame were pushed to black. Spot metering rendered a dramatic image.

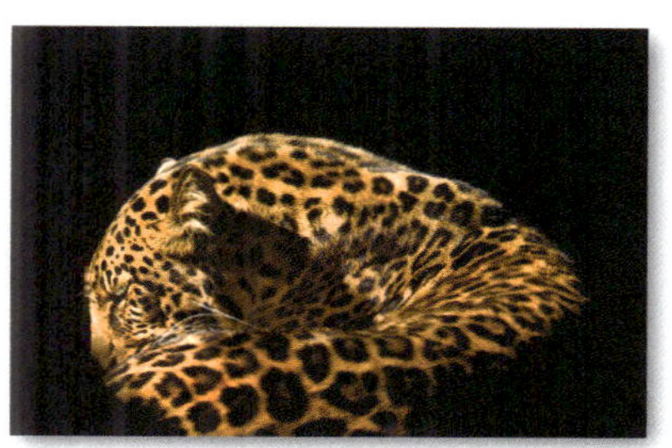

5) White Balance

White balance adjusts for lighting in order to make white objects appear white in photos. Once this calibration has been done, the camera correctly displays other colors. The chart below shows the white balance setting options. Before you begin photographing, choose the white balance setting that matches the light source. The setting you choose serves as the basis for color correction. For outdoor wildlife photography, use the daylight, cloudy or shade setting.

Change your white balance setting when you move indoors or use flash.

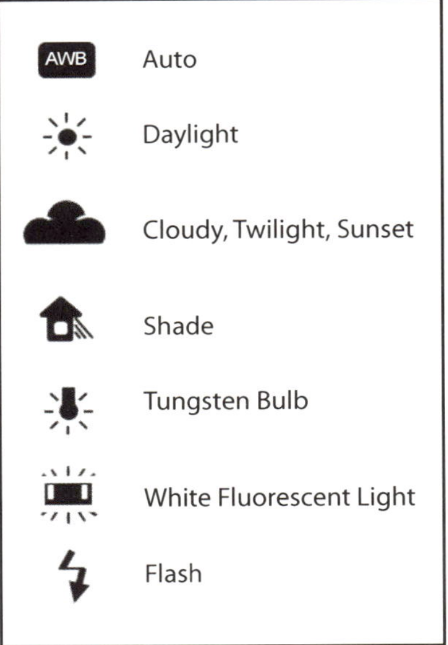

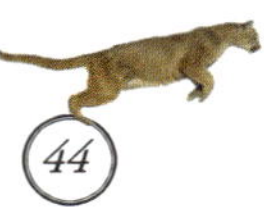

6) Exposure Compensation

As noted before, exposure meters are designed to give exposure readings perceptually in the middle between white and black. As long as your subject is not very light or very dark, the camera will render a proper exposure. Of course, not all subjects fall into a medium gray or medium color range. This is where exposure compensation is very helpful, but only when using in Aperture Priority or Shutter Speed Priority exposure modes.

Exposure compensation enables you to preset +/- adjustment that will be applied after the camera has metered the frame. You are basically adding or subtracting light from the camera's setting. When in Shutter Speed Priority, the f-stop will be changed by the adjustment amount you set. When in Aperture Priority, the shutter speed will be changed by the adjustment amount you set.

For example, when photographing an Arctic Fox in the snow, the camera's meter will make the exposure darker to bring it closer to middle gray. To compensate, you will need to adjust the exposure compensation up to +2 stops. It may seem counter intuitive, but you are telling the camera that you want the Arctic Fox to be brighter than middle gray.

Arctic Fox
Shutter Speed Priority Mode
Aperture: f/7
Shutter Speed: 1/640s
ISO: 800
Lens Focal Length: 200mm
Exposure Compensation: +1.7

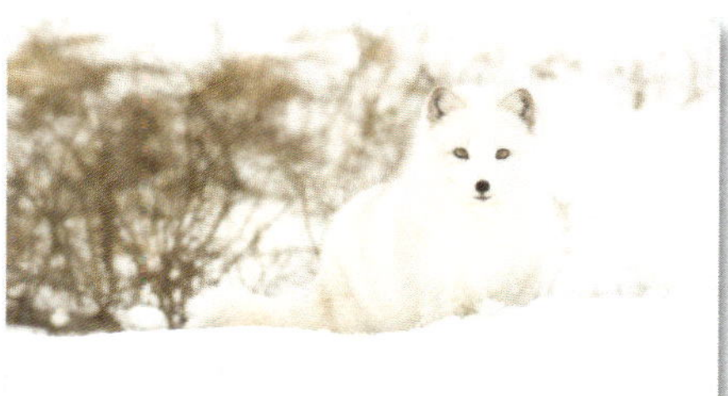

Conversely, if you are photographing a black bear, you will need to adjust the exposure compensation down 1 to 2 stops. In this example, the camera will try to brighten the tone of the bear; and with exposure compensation, you are indicating that the bear needs to be darker.

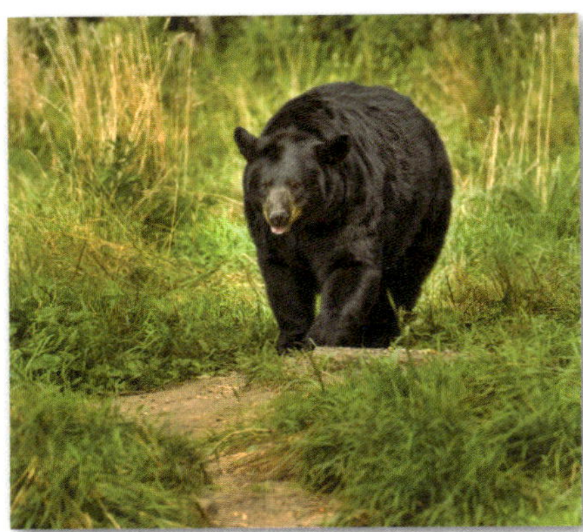

Black Bear
Shutter Speed Priority Mode
Aperture: f/6.3
Shutter Speed: 1/400s
ISO: 800
Lens Focal Length: 200mm
Exposure Compensation: -1.0

Histogram

The histogram is a graphic representation of the range of tones from dark to light in a photo, and it will tell you instantly if all parts of the scene are recorded by the sensor.

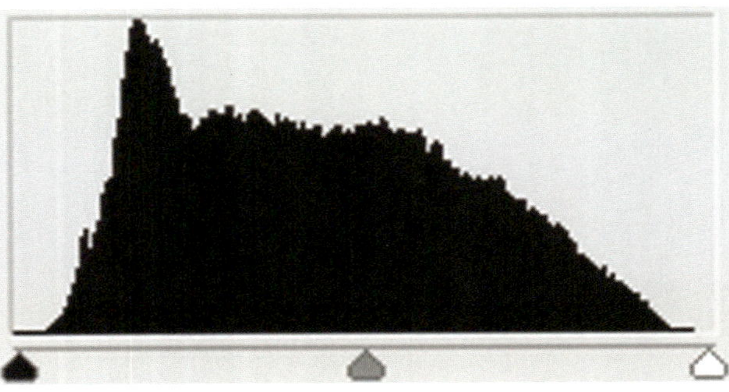

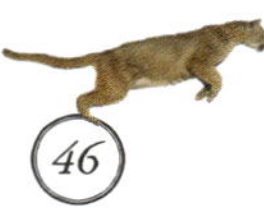

To retain detail and color in highlight (bright) areas and shadow (dark) areas, the histogram should drop to zero before reaching either side of the graph's edge. If the curve touches either side of the graph, detail is being lost and cannot be recovered. It is an indication that exposure *may* need to be adjusted.

If the histogram is pushed to left, you may need to adjust shutter speed, aperture, ISO or exposure compensation to add light. If the histogram is pushed to the right, you may need to adjust shutter speed, aperture, ISO or exposure compensation to reduce light. In most situations, an ideal histogram will not be clipped on either side.

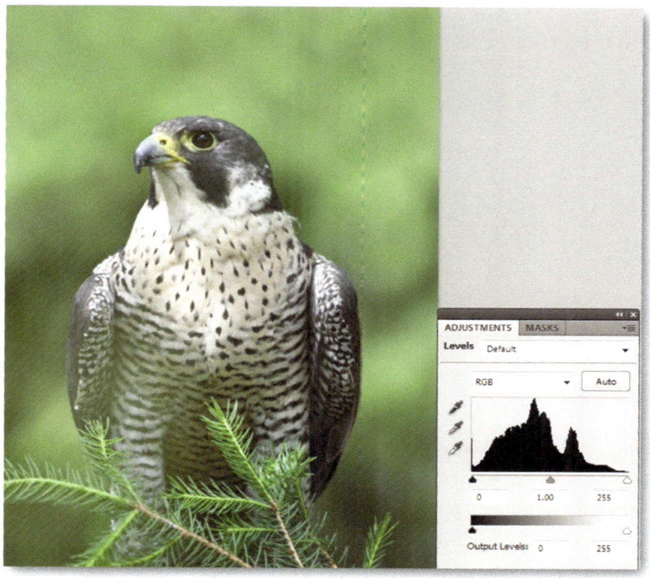

Histogram Examples

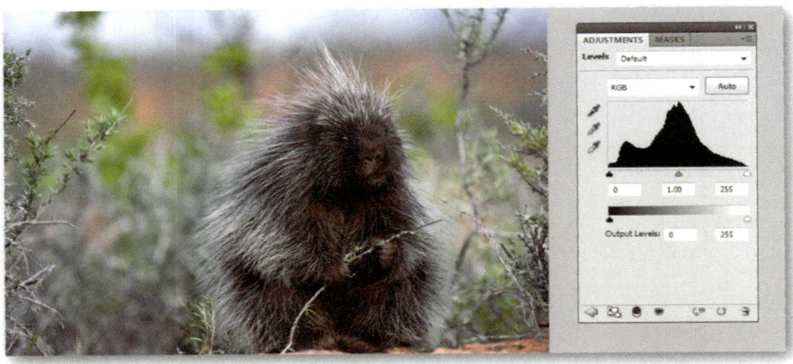

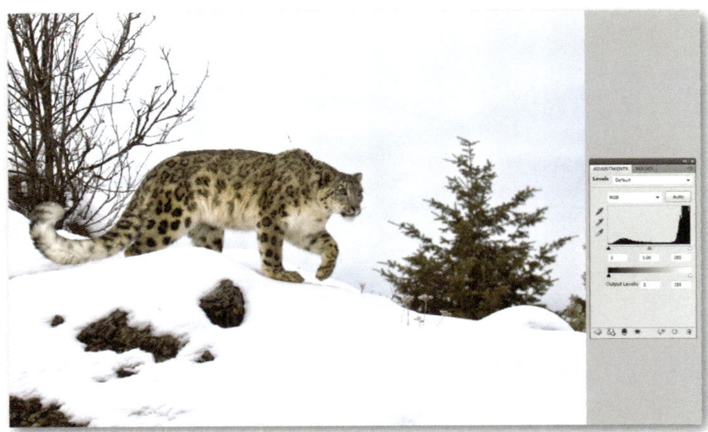

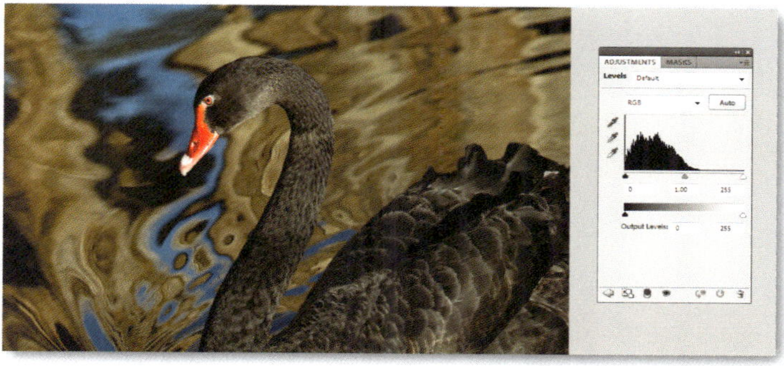

Blinkies

Most cameras have a setting that notifies the photographer when they are overexposing the image (too much light). It is commonly called "blinkies." When you review the image, you might see white flashes blinking on and off. This means detail is lost and cannot be recovered in the area that is blinking. Similar to the results of reviewing the histogram, when there are blinkies, exposure may need to be adjusted.

7) **Auto Focus Settings**

There are specific camera settings and equipment factors that influence sharpness of the subject and the overall photograph. This section explains depth of field and how to get the most value from the camera's auto focus functions.

Depth of Field (DOF)

Depth of Field is how much of a given photograph is in sharp focus, from foreground to background. Only the subject you are focused on is razor sharp. Other elements in front of and behind the subject will be somewhat sharp. "Shallow" depth of field means a limited part of the photo is in sharp focus. "Extensive" depth of field means most or all of the photo is in sharp focus.

The following factors control depth of field:

a) Focal Length - A long lens (such as 300-600mm) produces shallow depth of field. A short lens (such as 28-35mm) produces extensive depth of field. A telephoto lens enables you to get closer, isolate the subject from its surroundings, compress the scene, and is great for wildlife portraits.

b) Subject Distance - As you get closer to the subject, depth of field decreases to fractions of an inch.

c) Focus Point - Depth of field extends about 1/3 in front of the focus point, and 2/3 behind it. Focus on the eye of the tiger and its nose will be in focus. When photographing an animal with a long face, such as a zebra or wolf, try to photograph their profile to ensure their eye or nose is in sharp focus.

d) Aperture (f-stop) - Small f-stops such as f/4, produce limited depth of field. Large f-stops such as f/22, increase the zone of what is in sharp focus.

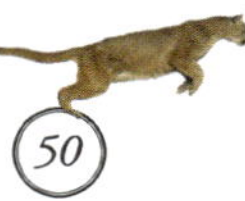

If your camera has a depth-of-field preview button, press and hold it to check the actual depth of field before you press the shutter.

This makes the image very dark in the viewfinder, but it shows how the background sharpness changes as you make adjustments.

Auto Focus Mode

Use Auto Focus (versus Manual focus) for most wildlife photography, because there is rarely sufficient time to compose and manually focus a wildlife photo. Cameras offer the following two types of autofocus modes by which the camera focuses automatically when the shutter-release button is pressed halfway.

a) Single Servo (S) or One Shot AF Mode - When the shutter-release button is pressed halfway, the auto focus function focuses and locks.

Use Single Servo (S) or One Shot AF Mode when the subject occupies a very small area of the frame or when the subject is the same color as the background.

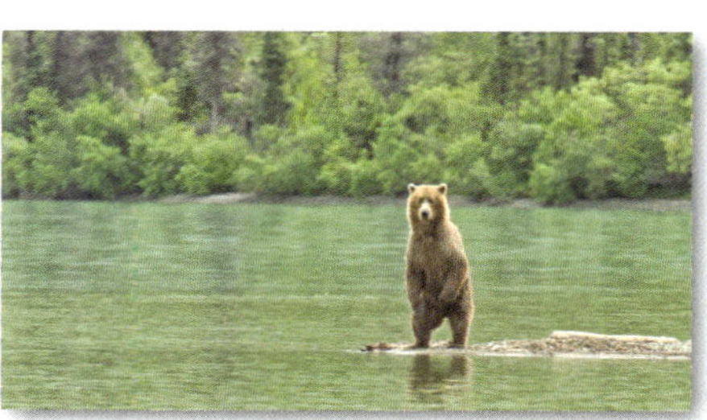

b) **Continuous Servo (C) or AI Servo Mode -** The auto focus function focuses continuously while the shutter-release button is pressed halfway. If the subject moves, the camera will engage predictive focus tracking to predict the final distance to subject and adjust focus as necessary. For most wildlife photography, use Continuous Servo (AI Servo) mode.

Auto Focus Area Mode

Focus points are the little empty squares or dots that you see when you look through your viewfinder. The area of the frame that the camera will use for auto focus is shown by the focus points. The robustness and flexibility of auto focus is primarily a result of the number, position and type of auto focus points made available by a given camera model. Read and understand your camera's options. Here are general descriptions of Auto Focus Area Modes.

a) **Single Point or Manual AF Point -** The camera uses *one focus point* that you choose in your viewfinder to acquire focus. Use Single Point Mode for the majority of wildlife photography, because it enables you to focus on a specific feature such as an animal's eyes.

b) Dynamic Area or AF Point Expansion - Choose one focus point. Once focus is acquired, if your subject moves, the camera will utilize the surrounding focus points to track subject movement and keep the focus on your subject. Pan the camera along with the subject to make sure the subject stays close to the initially-selected focus point.

Use Dynamic Area (or AF Point Expansion) and/or Predictive (3D) Tracking for wildlife that is running, flying or moving sporadically.

To track a small portion of the scene, pick a small number of points (such as 9 points).

To track the entire frame, pick the highest number of points available or predictive (3D) tracking to track your subject.

c) Auto Area or Auto Point Selection - This is the "point-and-shoot" method whereby the camera selects the focus point. *This option is not recommended because it takes away your control.*

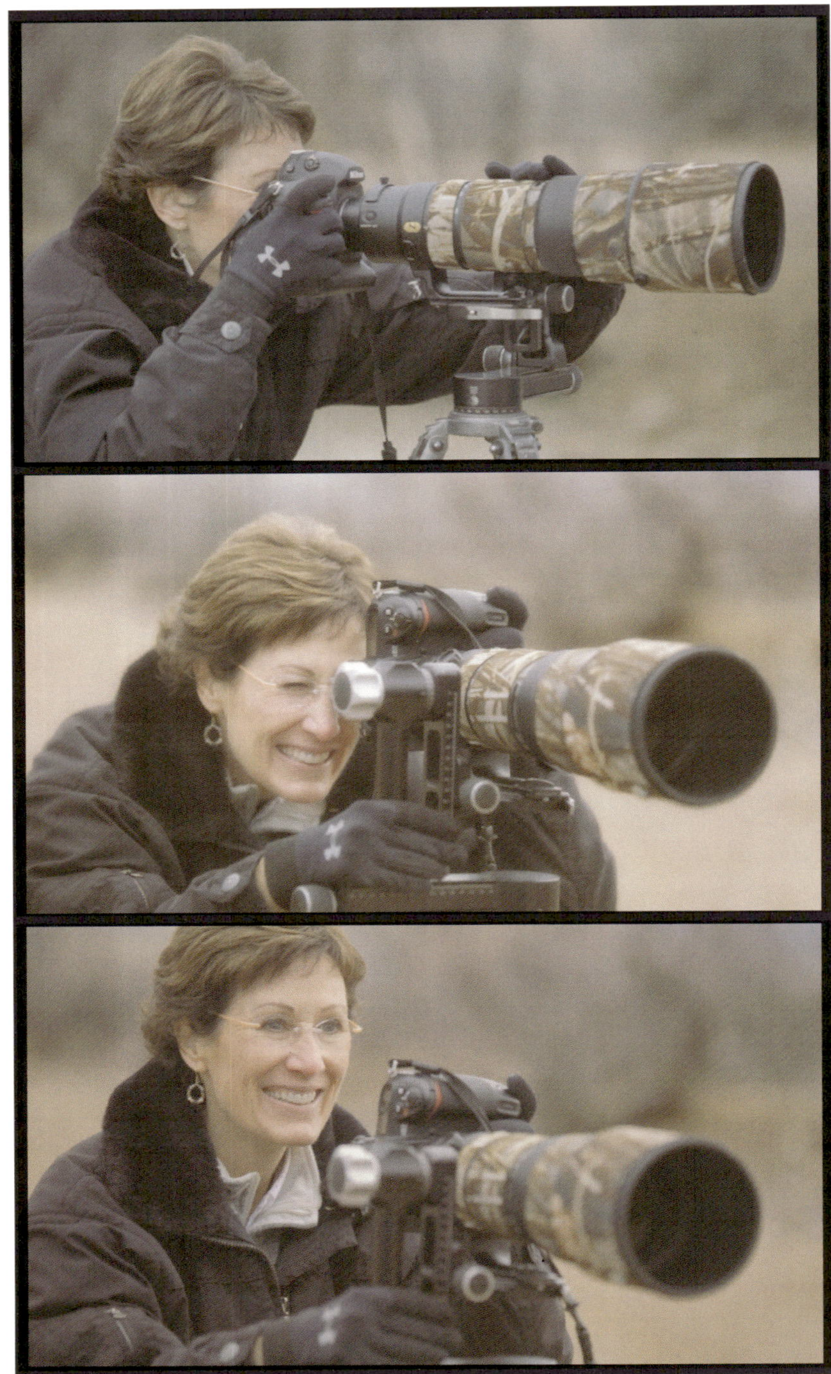

Photos by Christopher Orrett

Setting Up on Location

This section covers the following and will help you maximize the experience of being on location:

1) Stabilizing the Camera
2) Photographing through a Wire Fence
3) Photographing through Plexiglas®
4) Additional Photography Tips

1) Stabilizing the Camera

a. Your car is a terrific blind for watching and photographing wildlife. If you stop and park, be sure to pull completely off the road and park in designated areas. Use a bean bag on the windowsill on which to stabilize your camera and lens.

b. When using a tripod or monopod, leave the tripod's pan and tilt controls loose enough so you can follow-focus the subject. You will get sharper photos this way than if you try to handhold the camera.

c. Avoid extending the center post of a tripod, because it is less stable. Hang your bag as a weight from the center hook to further stabilize the tripod.

d. A gimbal head (pivot) on the tripod works best for birds or when you need to pan the movement.

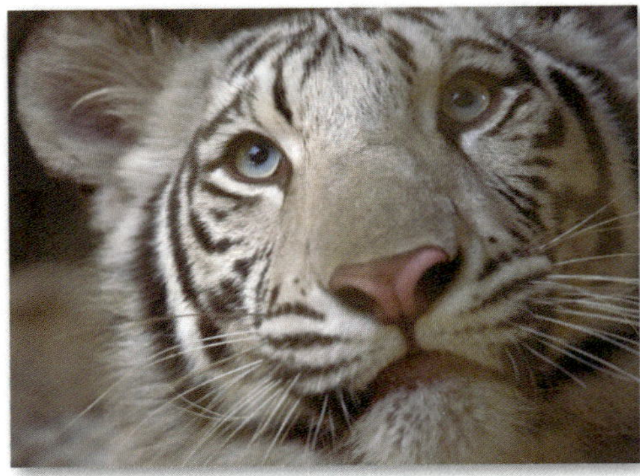

Bengal Tiger
Aperture: f/6.3
Shutter Speed: 1/125s
ISO: 2000
Lens Focal Length: 500mm

Effect: Tripod for slow shutter speed, high ISO for low light conditions

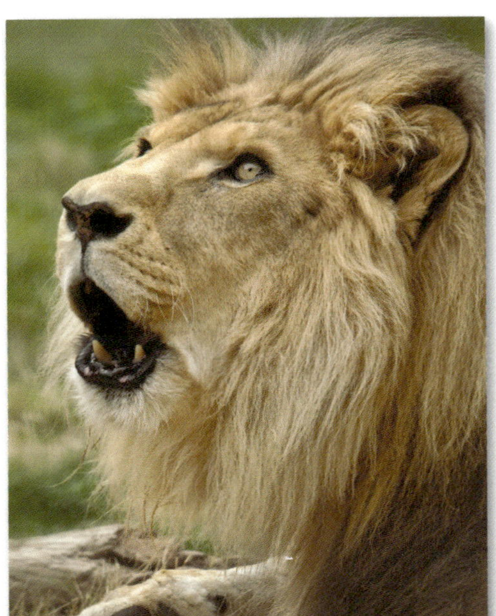

African Lion
Aperture: f/6
Shutter Speed: 1/500s
ISO: 400
Lens Focal Length: 525mm

Effect: Small f-stop and long focal length made the fence disappear

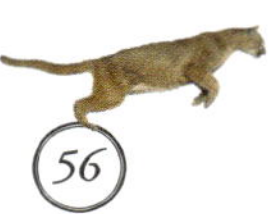

e. When it is not possible to use a tripod or monopod, and you must handhold the camera, have one hand supporting the lens from underneath while the other hand operates the camera's controls and shutter. Keep your elbows tucked tight against your body. Always look for ways to brace yourself against your own body or a fixed structure.

f. Take a test photo of the scene to check your exposure.

2) Photographing through a Wire Fence

a. Use a telephoto lens, the longer the better. If you are able to put the lens close to the fence, a 100mm lens will work. The farther you are away from the fence, the longer the telephoto lens you will need to make the fence disappear. (It disappears because it is so out of focus.) Generally, if you are a few feet away from the fence, then a 400-600mm focal length will be necessary.

b. Use a large lens opening - maximum or widest possible aperture (f/2.8 – f/6.3). A shallow depth of field will make the fence disappear.

c. Place the lens as close to the fence as possible and focus on the distant subject. The animal must be away from the fence to make the fence disappear.

d. Do not use a flash.

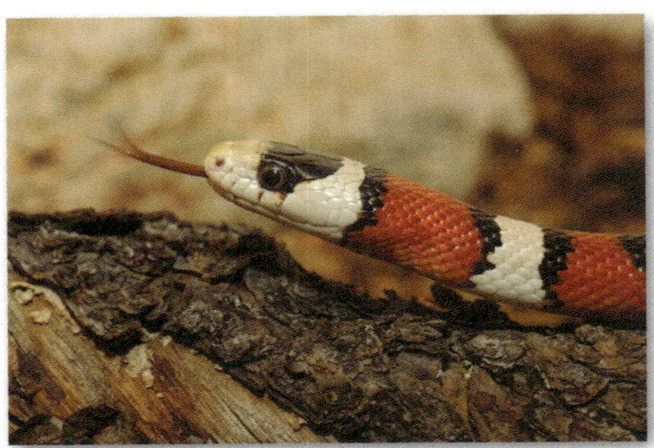

Sonoran Mountain Snake
Through Plexiglas
Using Single Flash
Aperture: f/16
Shutter Speed: 1/250s
ISO: 200
Lens Focal Length: 105mm

Effect: Shutter speed synchronized to the flash, high f-stop provided good depth of field

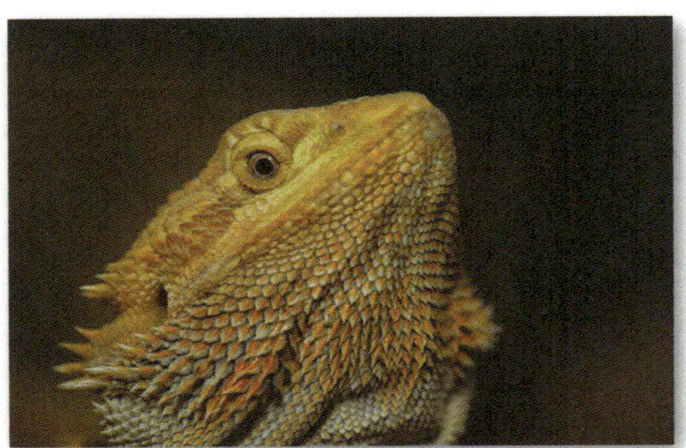

Iguana
Through Plexiglas
Using Single Flash
Aperture: f/9
Shutter Speed: 1/250s
ISO: 800
Lens Focal Length: 105mm

Effect: Relatively small f-stop rendered only the eyes in sharp focus

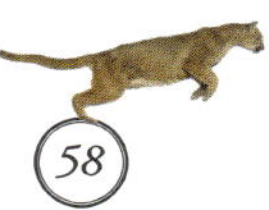

3) Photographing through Plexiglas®

a. Use a flexible rubber lens hood to block stray light.

b. Pick a clean spot on the glass.

c. Place the lens hood directly on the glass. So you do not bang the glass, use your pinky finger on one hand to gently touch your lens to the glass.

d. Use a flash for illumination if allowed.

e. Use Manual Exposure Mode to calculate exposure manually.

4) Additional Photography Tips

a. Always be ready with your camera. Sometimes you will get the picture on the way to your destination, so be flexible!

b. Take verticals and horizontals. Try different compositions.

c. Keep the camera level with the horizontal plane.

d. Take a range of photos of your subject. Take a portrait photo, then one with the general habitat in context to the subject, then another with close-up detail.

Final Note from the Author

People attend my photography workshops with varied levels of expertise, but they all take away something to advance their wildlife photography. It does not matter where you are on your journey; be patient and forgiving with yourself. What matters is that you discover animal behavior, photograph often, review your results, study your camera functions and continue to refine your technique to improve the outcome.

Though there are many guidelines in this book, I want you to remember that creating extraordinary photographs comes from applying the guidelines, but finding our own style. Most importantly, enjoy the personal connections with wildlife and capturing those incredible moments.

Be sure to visit KathleenReeder.com for updated resources and upcoming workshops.

Keep at it!
Kathleen Reeder

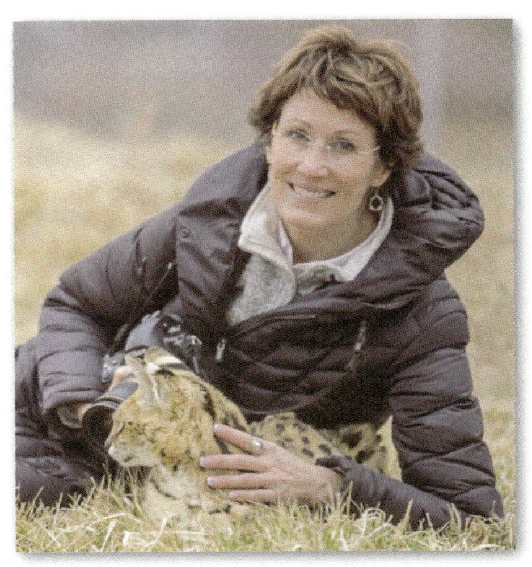

Photo by Christopher Orrett

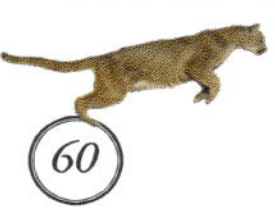

About the Author

KATHLEEN REEDER is an internationally-published, award-winning wildlife photographer extraordinaire. Her works reflect her personality: passionate, energetic, adventurous and focused. A sensitive eye and an intimate relationship with her subjects are the signatures of her work. She is a highly-accomplished professional with an eager desire to share her knowledge with photographers of all skill sets.

Kathleen's marvelous work has appeared on NBC's The Today Show, and has been highlighted in newspapers, magazines and on internet sites including, National Geographic, New York Daily News, HELLO! Magazine, The Sun, Daily Telegraph News, Mail Online World News, Arizona Highways Magazine, and Arizona Game and Fish Wildlife Views.

Ms. Reeder resides in Arizona and travels throughout the world to photograph the wild spirit that still survives. Using her expert photographic techniques, she captures the expression, emotional impact and spiritual essence of wild animals. Kathleen believes, "Whether you are an amateur or professional photographer, the opportunity is all around us to take extraordinary wildlife photos."

Follow Kathleen Reeder Wildlife Photography on Facebook where she regularly shares many of her camera settings, tips and set-up details behind her spectacular iamges; or attend one of her much-revered live workshops.

View and purchase all of her amazing photographs at:
KathleenReeder.com

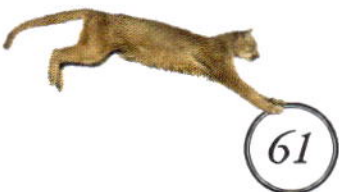

ACKNOWLEDGEMENTS

I would like to acknowledge the following individuals for making this book a reality. No matter if it was a small gesture of support or a significant addition to the work, please know that you are genuinely appreciated.

Ranee Alison
Susan Blais
Carol Budrow
Rodney Cervantes
Peg Coleman
Jay Deist
Bonnie Evans
Alan Feldman
Sharon Fenderson
Laura Flannigan
Jennifer Firmage-Stamness
Prayeri Harrison
Dean Harrison
Edward Harry
Jeff Harwell
Wayne Johnson
Lisa Kazanjian
Roberta Lites
Laura McLane
Mark Mikelat
Peter Mortimer
Kathleen O'Neil
Christopher Orrett
Courtney Palmer
Marilou Peavley
Dean Powell
Ashton Powell
Sydney Raitano
Bernice Reeder
John Reeder/Dee Denny
Jim Ryder
Lynn Sankey
Michael Sankey
Kyle Schlegel
Haig Tchamitch
Mary Therese Veile

Thank You! :)

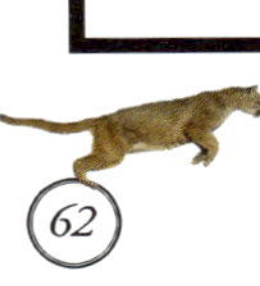

INDEX

NOTES

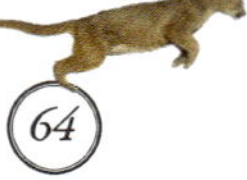

CPSIA information can be obtained at www.ICGtesting.com
Printed in the USA
LVIW01n1120100915
453441LV00001B/1